NOT HEARERS ONLY
VOLUME III

Bible Studies in the Epistle of James

JOHN BLANCHARD

WORD BOOKS
LONDON

Published by Word Books, London, a
Division of Word (UK) Ltd., Park Lane,
Hemel Hempstead, Hertfordshire.

ISBN 0 85009 045 8

Made and printed in Great Britain by
Hunt Barnard Printing Ltd.,
Aylesbury, Bucks.

TO JOYCE

FOREWORD

by The Rev. Dr. Raymond Brown, PhD., MA., B.D., M.Th.

Christians who have read John Blanchard's two previous books in this series will be eager to read this equally helpful volume. Here is an enriching exposition of the fourth chapter of James's down-to-earth, practical New Testament epistle.

Our Christianity is nothing if it is not related to everyday life, and the Epistle of James makes sure that our daily conduct is consistent with our doctrinal conviction. Yet Martin Luther once described the Epistle of James as 'an epistle of straw'. He was wrong, of course, for there is nothing 'strawy' about it, but to be fair to him he claimed to be comparing it with 'books that show you Christ'. He was naturally fascinated by the superb teaching of such epistles as Romans and Galatians, and turned to James looking for an exposition of similar themes.

But a closer look reveals that the Epistle of James *does* 'show you Christ'. It shows you Christ the matchless Teacher, and is full of fascinating allusions to the Lord's own teaching in the Sermon on the Mount and elsewhere. How can it possibly be 'straw' when its message is of such supreme importance? No, here is food, not straw, and John Blanchard is a most reliable guide and exponent. I have greatly enjoyed reading this book and am sure that this gifted expository and devotional treatment will be of immence help to many.

Martin Luther's comment about 'an epistle of straw' comes from his *Preface to the New Testament*. He is a more helpful guide in his *Preface to the Epistle of James*, where he says 'I praise it, and consider it a good book because it sets up no doctrine of man but vigorously promulgates the law of God.' That's better! I join with others in thanking Mr. Blanchard for his fine insights into the message of this 'good book'.

RAYMOND BROWN
AUGUST 1973.

PREFACE

The Epistle of James has always had a peculiar fascination for me, ever since I first 'discovered' it soon after my conversion. From then on I have been drawn to it again and again. It was one of the first parts of the Bible I went through as a Bible Class leader at Holy Trinity Church, Guernsey in 1958, using, I remember, Canon Guy King's book 'A Belief that Behaves' as a general basis. Later, when I travelled to England as a member of a parish mission team, the Vicar of the Church involved based his daily ministry to the team on the same Epistle, and I began to gain new insights into this great little book.

Some years afterwards, as a staff evangelist with the National Young Life Campaign, I dug a little deeper as I studied it in series with several NYLC branches in the West Country. Then in 1966, on the staff of the Movement for World Evangelization, I led the first of what has since become a large number of delightfully happy house-parties in Europe and elsewhere. Yet again I felt irresistibly drawn to the Epistle of James as a basis for the morning Bible Hour, and I found myself returning to the text with a new enthusiasm to discover fresh truths from the familiar words.

In the Autumn of 1968 I accepted an invitation to write a series of Bible Studies for 'Sunday Companion', and found great joy in re-shaping material on the first chapter of James to meet the particular demands of 1,000-word articles for 29 weeks. Those articles, later translated for use in Eastern Europe, greatly added to requests I was already receiving to consider producing a devotional study on the whole Epistle of James in more permanent form. In answering those requests, it was initially planned to prepare three volumes, of which this was to have been the last, but the third and fourth chapters of James's Epistle were found to contain such a wealth of material that it became necessary to extend the work to four volumes, of which this is the third.

Anyone even vaguely familiar with the New Testament knows the general line of the Epistle of James, and a glance at some of the titles of books devoted to it confirms the assessment that is made – 'The Behaviour of Belief' (Spiros Zodhiates), 'A Belief that Behaves' (Guy H. King), 'Make Your Faith Work' (Louis H. Evans), 'Faith that Works' (John L. Bird), 'The Tests of Faith' (J. Alec Motyer). These titles are all trying to crystallize the same truth, that James is a *practical* book, dealing with everyday life for the man in the street. Yet it is not devoid of doctrine, as we shall see when we begin to dig into the text. As Alec Motyer puts it, '. . . the distinctive value of James is his striking grasp of the integration of truth and life'. I agree! – and it is precisely this integration of truth and life that makes James so relevant today. Even as Christians we seem to have an almost incurable tendency to be unbalanced. We either major on accumulating truth, to the neglect of enthusiastic action, or we dash around in a mad whirl of activity, to the neglect of faith and truth. James provides just the balance we need. It is said that when a student was once asked to name his favourite translation of the Bible he replied 'My mother's'. 'Is it a translation into English?', his friend went on. 'No', he replied, 'it is a translation into action!' That, in a nutshell, is James's great concern.

In these studies, I have not sought to deal with critical and technical issues, which are beyond both my aim and my ability. I have therefore assumed, for instance, that the writer of the Epistle was 'James, the Lord's brother' (Galatians 1.19) and that it was written at some time between A.D. 45 and A.D. 62. I have simply come to the Word of God with an open heart and sought the Holy Spirit's help in understanding and applying it. In preparing these studies for publication in this form, I have sought, by use of the second person, to retain as much as possible of the personal thrust of the spoken word.

I would like to repeat my thanks to the Council of the Movement for World Evangelization for the privilege of serving the Movement in the ministry of the Word of God, and to Word (UK) Limited for their kind offer to publish these studies. I am also most grateful to Dr. Raymond

Brown for his kindness in writing such a generous Foreword. Finally, I am once again indebted to Miss Sheila Hellberg, who has typed and re-typed the manuscript with such faithfulness and accuracy.

My prayer for this third volume remains the same as for the first two, that the Lord will help writer and reader alike to obey His own clear command, given through James, to be 'doers of the word, and *not hearers only*'!

Croydon,   JOHN BLANCHARD
Surrey.
August, 1973

CONTENTS

Chapter 1

THE ROOT OF THE TROUBLE – I

*'From whence come wars and fightings among you?
come they not hence, even of your lusts that war in
your members?'* (James 4:1)

As even those with only a superficial understanding of the
Bible will realise, its division into chapters and verses was
not part of its original form. These were added many years
after even the last of the New Testament books was written,
and while the choice of numbering and division at times has
a wonderful sense of 'rightness' about it, we must not treat
it as infallible, or allow it to interrupt the flow of the writer's
original argument.

The end of James 3 and the beginning of James 4 may
perhaps provide us with a good illustration of what I mean,
for while our anonymous editor has decreed that we should,
as it were, turn over a new page after the words 'them that
make peace' (James 3:18), there is, in fact, a direct link
between those words and the opening words of James 4,
which are now before us. The link is the very obvious one
of contrast. Chapter 3 ends with the words 'And the fruit of
righteousness is sown in peace of them that make peace';
chapter 4 begins with the words 'From whence come wars
and fightings among you? come they not hence, even of your
lusts that war in your members?' In other words James is
contrasting the *ideal* (the practice of peace) with the *actual*
(a state of war), and having set before his readers the aim,
attitude and approach that should characterise the Christian,
he turns to demonstrate how far short they fall. We shall not
be long before discovering how relevant his findings are to
our 20th Century situation! Two headings will sum up the
contents of this verse. Notice –

1. *THE CONDITION HE DIAGNOSED* – 'From whence
come wars and fightings among you?'

This is the condition that James diagnosed as he looked

at the world of his day and in particular at the lives of his readers – 'wars and fightings among you'. Far from being peacemakers, working together in a spirit of peace, and producing a harvest of righteousness in their own lives and the lives of others, men were warring and fighting on every hand. In this little phrase James may be pointing out three things.

(1) *Something that was general.* – 'From whence come wars . . . ?' That word 'wars' comes from the Greek word *'stratos'*, meaning 'an encamped army'. It is a phrase used to illustrate a continuous state of war. Now as soon as he grasps that, the word begins to have an obvious relevance to the Christian. To show what I mean, notice these other scriptures containing the same basic word *'stratos'*. – 'We do not war after the flesh' (2 Corinthians 10:3); – 'war a good warfare' (1 Timothy 1:18) – in other words, continue throughout your life to fight this good warfare; 'abstain from fleshly lusts, which war against the soul' (1 Peter 2:11) – in other words, that continually war, that never cease warring, that are in a continual state of war, against the soul. So what James is saying right at the beginning of this part of his letter is this – 'Don't you know there's a war on? Just look around you! There is a continuous state of war'. Was he right? If we are correct in assuming that the James who wrote this letter was the half-brother of Jesus, and if we have the right date for the letter (somewhere between AD 45 and AD 62), then it was probably written in Jerusalem, where James lived from the time of the resurrection of Jesus until he was martyred some 30 years later. Now the interesting thing about that very distinct possibility is that the name 'Jerusalem' probably means 'the city of peace'. Certainly the Hebrew word for peace is *'shalom'*, and the first part of the city's name may mean 'possession' or 'foundation'. Jerusalem! The city of peace! But that was only its name, and not its experience. Quite apart from its long and bloody Old Testament history, it was invaded by Antiochus IV about 168 BC, Judas the Maccabee led a revolt there a few years later, Roman forces overthrew it in 63 BC and again in 54 BC, the Parthians plundered it in 40 BC, and Herod the Great fought a fierce battle for its possession in 37 BC. The most recent

of these battles would have been fought while the parents of James's readers were alive – but it was also written at a time when the ferment of Jewish revolt was boiling up all over again, a ferment leading to its invasion by the Roman Emperor Titus in the year AD 70. In that particular invasion 1,100,000 people were killed and the Temple and fortifications destroyed once more. That gives us the background against which James wrote of 'wars' – a continuous state of unrest. But was that just a word for those days? Did the centuries after that bring any change in the state of the world? In his book 'The Study of War', Professor Quincey examines the period from 1480 to 1941 and says that in that period of 461 years, these nations were engaged in the following number of major wars:– Great Britain 78, France 71, Spain 64, Russia 61, Austria 52, Germany 23, the United States of America 13, China 11 and Japan 9. What astonishing figures! Today, in the second half of the 20th Century, we have had to invent a new phrase, 'the cold war', to describe the continuous state of international tension. Speaking at the United Nations on 26th September 1961, USA President John F. Kennedy said 'Every man, woman and child lives under a nuclear sword of Damocles, hanging by the slenderest of threads, capable of being cut at any moment by accident, miscalculation or madness'. To ensure a 'balance of power' the USA possesses enough aerosol nerve gas to kill all living matter on an area eight times the size of the globe on which we live! Two thousand years ago, Jesus prophesied that there would be a time of 'wars and rumours of wars' (Matthew 24:6). If ever such a time existed upon the face of the earth, it exists now, and it makes James's words grippingly relevant in today's world. But James not only had in mind something that was general. He also mentioned

(2) *Something that was individual*. He speaks not only of 'wars' but of 'wars and fightings'. It may be that the original language of this verse should literally have been translated as a rather more extended phrase, or even as two separate questions, so that it would have read something like this – 'From whence come wars? And from whence come fightings among you?' At least the word 'fightings' is quite different in meaning from the word 'wars'. It means individual con-

flicts rather than a general, continuous state of war. The
Amplified Bible translates it 'conflicts, quarrels and fightings'. It may be that in adding this phrase James is narrow-
ing the issue down from the international level or even
national level and bringing it home to the lives of his individual readers. One thing is certain: even the greatest of wars
in the history of the world began with individual people.
What is more, the longest wars in the world have all begun
with a single battle. And there is a deeply personal application of that which we dare not miss! If the fiercest, the
bloodiest, the costliest wars have begun with one man's
festered heart; if the longest wars have begun with a single
battle; dare we ever behave in such a way that we are the
people who in our homes, in our places of work, in our
churches, in our organisations, in our social, community or
political spheres, begin that continuous state of war, or strike
that first blow that can lead to so much misunderstanding,
misery, pain, suffering, injury and sorrow? There is something individual here. James is not indulging in idle theory.

Something general, something individual. But notice a
third thing –

(3) *Something shameful.* – 'From whence come wars and
fightings among *you*?' The italics belong to me, but I am
sure the intention belonged to James! You see, he was
writing to Christians, to those who claimed to have found
what the Bible calls 'the way of peace' (Luke 1:79) – yet they
were obviously fighting and squabbling and in a state of
unrest. Surely that was a shameful thing, that Christian
people should be tearing themselves apart? And that kind
of thing did go on from time to time in the early church. We
must not make the mistake of thinking that the early church
was a perfect model of Christian living! Look at these scriptures, for instance – Paul wrote to the church at Philippi, 'I
beseech Euodias, and beseech Syntyche, that they be of the
same mind in the Lord'. (Philippians 4:2) These two Christians were obviously at loggerheads over something or other.
To the church at Corinth Paul wrote '. . . it has been reported
to me by Chloe's people that there is quarrelling among you'
(1 Corinthians 1:11 RSV); and a little further on, 'When one
of you has a grievance against a brother, does he dare go to

THE ROOT OF THE TROUBLE – I

law before the unrighteous instead of the saints?' (1 Corinthians 6:1 RSV); and in a later letter, 'For I fear that perhaps I may come and find you not what I wish . . . that perhaps there may be quarrelling, jealousy, anger, selfishness, slander, gossip, conceit and disorder'. (2 Corinthians 12:20 RSV).

What a catalogue of contention! Is it not shameful to find that sort of behaviour amongst Christians? But before we condemn the Corinthians, let us examine our *own* churches, our *own* fellowships, *and our own hearts!* Are we without sin in this area? It is shameful for Christians to be guilty of these things – yet some churches are riddled with it.

Somebody once told a story to illustrate our weaknesses here, and while it may have been invented for children, I am sure adults will be able to grasp its meaning! This is the version I remember. There was trouble in the carpenter's workshop, and the tools were having a row. One of them said, 'It's the hammer's fault. He is much too noisy. He must go'. 'No' said the hammer, 'I think the blame lies with the saw. He keeps going backwards and forwards all the time'. The saw protested violently. 'I'm not to blame. I think it's the plane's fault. His work is so shallow. Why, he just skims the surface all the time'. The plane objected. 'I think the real trouble lies with the screwdriver. He is always going round in circles'. 'Nonsense', retorted the screwdriver, 'the trouble really began with the ruler because he is always measuring other people by his own standards'. 'Nonsense', the ruler replied, 'I think our real problem is the sandpaper. He is always rubbing people up the wrong way'. 'Why pick on me?' said the sandpaper, 'I think you ought to blame the drill, he is so boring'. Just as the drill was about to protest, the carpenter came in, took off his jacket, put on his overalls and began to work. He was making a pulpit at the time and by the time he had finished he had used every one of those tools to fashion something from which the gospel was eventually preached to thousands of people.

That is just a fable, of course. But do not miss the point it makes! The Lord in His wonderful grace does use the imperfect instruments He has at His disposal, but we all have a solemn responsibility to 'strive for peace with all men' (Hebrews 12:14 RSV), or, as the Apostle Paul puts it, to 'be at peace among yourselves' (1 Thessalonians 5:13).

So far in this verse to James's readers, we have been tracing the condition he diagnosed. Now we come to the second part of the verse –

2. *THE CAUSE HE DISCOVERED* – '. . . come they not hence, even of your lusts that war in your members?'

James has already touched upon this by exposing two motives behind the false wisdom that tries to gain its own ends without God. Those two causes, which James deals with in verses 14 and 16 of chapter 3, are envy and selfish ambition. First of all he wrote 'But if ye have bitter envying and strife in your hearts, glory not, and lie not against the truth' (3:14), and then added 'For where envying and strife is, there is confusion and every evil work' (3:16). In this further stage of his diagnostic examination, Doctor James plunges his knife even deeper and discovers another root of trouble. His report is amazingly concise – '. . . come they not hence, even of your lusts that war in your members?' – yet in it he says four important things about the cause of the trouble.

(1) *It is pleasure-seeking* – 'your lusts'. So that we begin to understand the meaning right away, let me say that I am using the word 'pleasure-seeking' as an adjective and not a noun. The cause of the trouble James has diagnosed is a pleasure-seeking cause. The word 'lusts' transliterated from Greek to English would read 'hedonon', from which we get the words 'hedonism' and 'hedonistic'. It is a different word from the word 'lust' used in James 1:14, where we are told that in sinning a man is 'drawn away of his own lust, and enticed'. There, the word means 'desire'. Here, it means 'the gratification of desire'. It is the spirit that demands immediate, selfish satisfaction. Speaking of his country's teen-agers, a Pastor in the United States once told me 'They have not learnt the value of delayed gratification'. His point was that whatever they wanted they could get. It was only a matter of dollars and there was a plentiful supply of those.

James is exposing the tyranny of self-satisfaction – and it is a tyranny, as we shall see in a moment. But we must think this through very carefully, because remember the point that James is making, which is that this is a cause of

wars and fightings. Now how do we bring these two together?
A pleasure-seeking, hedonistic spirit of life maintains that if
a thing is enjoyable, it is good; if it is good I must have it,
and I must have it now. But why does that produce wars and
fightings? The reason, I suggest, is this – because we can
only ultimately please ourselves, satisfy all our desires, be
completely hedonistic *at the expense of other people*. Somebody has got to pay for it! It is one of the most astonishing
evidences of the fact of the sovereignty of God that in spite
of all the fallenness of the world, in spite of the fact that man
has completely turned his back on his Maker, in spite of the
fact that multitudes of modern men would say that the Bible
is now completely outdated and irrelevant, the fact of the
matter is that we cannot cast off restraint, run riot, please
ourselves and be completely hedonistic without a price
having to be paid. *And that price is almost always paid in
fractured relationships!* I take that to be one of the most
astonishing evidences that God is God, that this is His world,
that there are spiritual laws that man can only break at his
peril. For all of man's progress, knowledge, success and
sophistication, he cannot please himself without somebody
paying a price. Is that not an astonishing thing? Here is a
man who says 'I am going to ignore God, the Bible, the
Church and religion in any shape or form. I am going to live
my life my way. I can afford to be extravagant, I can be
immoral without risk, I can indulge my every fancy, and
that is what I propose to do'. Now the terrifying thing is,
that when a man does that, there is a price to be paid – and
it is almost inevitable that part of the price to be paid is a
fracture in personal relationships. That is where the
advocates of our so-called 'permissive society' display the
most guilty ignorance of all. But there is more to it than that.
If we follow this hedonistic, 'I will please myself' line, we
automatically move God from the centre of the stage, and
dissipate the impact of His word. We can see this in the
parable of the sower in Luke 8, where we read that the seed
that fell among thorns was compared with those who are
'choked with cares and riches and *pleasures* (the same word
as 'lusts' in the verse we are studying) of this life' (Luke
8:14). Let me put it to you this way. If self-satisfaction

comes first, then, even at best, God can only come second, and when God comes second in a man's life he has problems! At a time when he was an athiest, Malcolm Muggeridge said 'The pursuit of happiness, however conceived, is the most foolish of all pursuits'. It is not only futile, but it is fatal too, because the parable about the seed closes up the verse from which we have quoted with the words 'and bring no fruit to perfection'. To put it in a nutshell, whenever you have seeking without finding, you have the ingredients of unrest and turmoil, or what James calls 'wars and fightings'.

This, then, is the first thing James says about the cause of the trouble. It is pleasure seeking.

(2) *It is persistent* – '. . . your lusts that war . . . '. You will remember the difference we noticed earlier in the verse between 'wars' and 'fightings'. The first was a continuous state of war, and the second an occasional specific skirmish or battle. Here, James goes back to the first word again – and it is exactly the right one to use. 'Your lusts that *war*' – that is, that carry on a continuous state of war. Here is one of a multitude of scriptures that militate very clearly against some interpretations of what has been called 'sinless perfection'. The fact of the matter is that each one of us has these lusts, these desires, this pleasure-seeking spirit of demanding instant satisfaction – and they never wholly leave us. The 20th Century New Testament translates this phrase, 'the desires which are always at war within you'. There is a continuous state of war going on in the heart and personality of every child of God. The Christian is a walking civil war. Professor R. V. G. Tasker says in the Tyndale New Testament Commentary, 'these pleasures are permanently on active service'. Our trouble is persistent! The 14th Century poet and humanist Francesco Petrarch once wrote 'Five great enemies to peace inhabit with us; avarice, ambition, envy, anger and pride. If these enemies were to be banished we should infallibly enjoy perfect peace'. But the sober truth is that they will never be permanently banished from our hearts this side of heaven. The enemy is entrenched within us and will fight to the last gasp. It is persistent! Let me add just one other comment. In our frantic 20th Century, which

makes such tremendous demands on our time, our skills and our nervous and physical energies, it is perhaps a natural corollary that pleasure for pleasure's sake should be one of the universal creeds of our generation. In terms of application, responsibility and pressure of many kinds, the demands made upon us today are perhaps greater than those made upon any previous generation. It is perhaps little wonder that, at the same time, we should have an explosion of the doctrine of pleasure for pleasure's sake. Let us be aware of the danger!

Now James turns to a third point about the cause of our trouble –

(3) *It is personal* – '. . . your lusts that war in *your* members'. James is not talking arid theory here. Nor is he contrasting the world with the church. Nor is he naming certain backsliders and pinpointing their particular trouble. He is identifying a factor common to all Christians. We cannot escape here into the orthodoxy of our theology or the success of our church. This is a personal issue – '*your* lusts that war in *your* members'. As I study it, this verse strikes me as an inverted triangle. First of all we have 'wars', which is a continuous state of unrest. Then we have 'fightings' which is a narrower thing, because it refers to individual skirmishes and battles. Then we have 'your lusts' that brings the matter even closer to heart. Finally we get the one word 'your', which brings me to the apex of the triangle, and that apex is like an arrow pointing straight at my heart, something from which I cannot escape.

Let me put it another way. The world consists of nations, nations consist of communities, communities consist of families, and families consist of individuals. Now it is so easy to moralise, to discuss doctrine, to pass judgment generally on things, to read the Word of God and draw the line of difference between good and evil, as general principles at large in the world. It is quite another thing to say the three little words, 'I have sinned'! When the prophet Nathan came to King David with the story of a rich man who stole a poor man's single ewe lamb in order to provide a meal for a guest, David had no problem in assessing the moral issue and in dispensing verbal judgment – Of course, I see what was wrong. 'As the Lord lives, the man who has done this deserves to die' (2 Samuel 12 : 5 RSV). It was so simple! An open and shut case. But when Nathan replied 'You are the man', David was shaken to the core. *You* are the man. You are guilty of the very sin you have condemned. The faithful and courageous Nathan then went on to bring God's word of condemnation right home to the King's heart, until David cried out 'I have sinned against the Lord'. Only then was Nathan able to bring the precious word of cleansing. 'The Lord also has put away your sin'. The lesson is surely clear. Beware of judging others and failing to recognise the subtle sin in your own heart. And remember, too, that these 'lusts' may not appear to be grossly sinful. They may even be camouflaged with the colours of legitimacy. But anything that comes before God is wrong.

Now to James's final point about the cause of our trouble –

(4) *It is penetrating* – 'your lusts that war in your *members*'. Now James is not speaking about the members of the church, but about the members' members! – what the Amplified Bible calls 'your bodily members'. Four centuries before Christ was born, the philosopher Plato said 'The sole cause of wars, and revolutions, and battles, is nothing other than the body and its desires'. But although Plato was a wise man, he only knew what the Apostle Paul calls 'the wisdom of the wise' (1 Corinthians 1 : 19), and he was a long way from the truth when he 'earthed' man's troubles in 'nothing other than the body and its desires'. He was making the mistake of saying that the body *in itself* was evil. But that is not what the Bible teaches. Let us be quite clear about that. The Bible does not teach that the body is an evil thing. You may have heard of the man who had engraved on his tombstone the words, 'Here lies the part of Thomas Wood that kept his soul from doing good'! That is very witty, very appealing – but totally unbiblical. The Bible does not teach that the body is the part of us that prevents us from doing good. That, incidentally, is a basic false assumption made by those who seek to elevate the spirit by starving the body or punishing it in some other way. When Paul says 'For the desires of the flesh are against the Spirit, and the desires of the Spirit are against the flesh' (Galatians 5 : 17 RSV), he

does not have in mind a contest between the physical and the spiritual. What he is speaking of is the conflict between the Christian's old nature and the Holy Spirit who now dwells within him. In other words, the Christian's body (incorporating all his personality and faculties) is not so much an evil, defiled thing – it is occupied territory.

I remember returning as a teenager to my native Guernsey, in the Channel Islands, after World War II. Everywhere I went there were signs of the German occupation – concrete bunkers, gun emplacements, German writing on walls and signposts, and so on, mute reminders of the fact that for five years the island was occupied territory. I was evacuated a few days before the invasion, but thousands of Guernseymen remained as the (then) enemy moved in. Now did they despise their native island because an enemy had penetrated it? Of course not. The island was still something very dear to them, something that they hallowed. It was occupied territory, but they cherished it, yearned for its welfare, and longed for its freedom. That is a far from perfect illustration, I know, but perhaps it will help in grasping the truth of what James is saying and in applying it to our own attitudes and actions. The cause of our trouble is not just outward, or external, or circumstantial. It is inward, personal and *penetrative* – 'in your members'.

In threading through this one verse with James, we have studied the condition that he diagnosed – 'wars and fightings among you', and the cause that he discovered – 'your lusts that war in your members', lusts that are pleasure-seeking, persistent, personal and penetrative. It would be natural to expect him to follow a condition and a cause with a cure. There is a cure, of course, but James does not begin to deal with it directly until verse 6. Before he does so, he has a great deal more to say about the sickness! However, in order to close this particular study on a positive note, rather than on a negative one, let me just say this: the only answer to persistent attack from an entrenched enemy engaging us in a continual state of war and penetrating every part of our personality, lies along the lines of persistent resistance and vigilance. Here, surely, is part of the scriptural answer to those who would claim that there is some kind of cataclysmic experience that a Christian can have, which puts him once and for all into a state where he is incapable of sinning, where he moves up from being a second-class Christian to being a first-class one. I must say, in all charity towards those who seem to hold these views that I do not find that taught anywhere in the Bible. What I find is that the greatest of men, at their highest spiritual moments, are nevertheless capable of committing the most terrible sins. If you study the Bible carefully you will find that some of the greatest of men, Jesus excepted, committed their greatest sin at their moments of greatest maturity. We must therefore be in a continuous state of vigilant prayerfulness, discipline and worship.

Charles Wesley, in one of his magnificent hymns, puts it like this:

> Leave no unguarded place,
> No weakness of the soul;
> Take every virtue, every grace,
> And fortify the whole:
> Indissolubly joined, to battle all proceed;
> But arm yourselves with all the mind
> That was in Christ, your Head.

Chapter 2

THE ROOT OF THE TROUBLE – II

'Ye lust, and have not: ye kill, and desire to have, and cannot obtain: ye fight and war, yet ye have not, because ye ask not. Ye ask, and receive not, because ye ask amiss, that ye may consume it upon your lusts'.

(James 4:2–3)

In these two verses, James continues to expose the root cause of 'wars and fightings' and indeed of a major part of fractured personal relationships, and moves on to emphasise just how deadly these things are and to show at least one way in which they adversely affect the Christian's daily walk. Two general headings sum up his description of the people to whom he wrote.

1. *THEIR PASSIONS WERE DESTRUCTIVE* – 'Ye lust, and have not: ye kill, and desire to have, and cannot obtain: ye fight and war . . .' (v. 2a) I have deliberately stopped the quotation there, because, as we shall see later, the remainder of this verse, and the whole of the next, hang together.

We are basing our studies on the wording of the Authorised Version, and to look at the wording and punctuation of this verse is to realise that somehow it seems awkward and clumsy. What I mean is this. The 'climax' words in the verse are obviously the words 'kill' and 'war'. They are clearly the two most serious words in the whole of the verse. There is a sort of progression of thought leading up to them. But the punctuation seems confusing, because there is a colon after the phrase 'ye lust and have not', but only a comma after the word 'kill'. This makes the phrase 'ye kill, and desire to have, and cannot obtain', seem even more odd, because once you have killed a thing, it is a bit late to start desiring to have it, and not obtaining it! Then we have another major break in the punctuation (a colon) before the final phrase 'ye fight and war'.

I hope that that does not all sound too technical and irrelevant, because I believe the key to the meaning of the verse lies in unravelling the punctuation. Originally, of course, there was no punctuation at all. James is not to blame for the commas and colons! Very simply, what we need to do is to discover a way of putting a break after the two climax words 'kill' and 'war'. If we did that the verse would begin to take on an orderly shape.

Now it so happens that there are at least three modern translations of this verse that follow the punctuation that I have suggested, and it will be helpful to quote all three; the first because it gives an amplified meaning of some of the words, the second because it has a very free flow about it, and the third because it is so concise. Bear in mind the punctuation that I have suggested and see if you can grasp the sense of what James is saying. The Amplified Bible says this – 'You are jealous and covet what others have and your desires go unfulfilled; so you become murderers. To hate is to murder as far as your hearts are concerned. You burn with envy and anger and are not able to obtain the gratification, the contentment and the happiness that you seek, so you fight and war'. Today's English Version (otherwise known as 'Good News for Modern Man') has this – 'You want things, but you cannot have them, so you are ready to kill; you covet things, but you cannot get them, so you quarrel and fight'. The Revised Standard Version puts it like this – 'You desire and do not have; so you kill. And you covet and cannot obtain; so you fight and wage war'. Technically, this kind of formula is called a parallelism – in other words the same thing said in two separate sets of words, which could be lined up parallel to or alongside each other.

In this case there are three groups of parallel or 'alongside' words. Firstly, 'Ye lust' and '(ye) desire to have'; secondly 'have not' and 'cannot obtain'; and thirdly 'ye kill' and 'ye fight and war'. Can you see the likeness between these three sets of phrases, and how the first two build up to the third? Now we have the verse ready for examination! As usual, James exhibits here a tremendously deep insight

into human nature. Notice this as we look more closely at
those three sets of phrases.

Firstly – the phrases 'ye lust' and '(ye) desire to have'. 'Ye
lust' could almost be translated, 'you set your heart and
mind on a thing'. Its meaning lies in the general area of
covetousness. The root of the second phrase is the Greek
word 'zelos', which is the word translated as 'envying' in
James 3:14 and 16. Here is the beginning of the trouble.
Just a thought, an idea. Then it becomes a strong feeling.
Later, it develops into a longing, and finally it flames into
a raging passion that fills the heart and the horizons of the
mind. A very similar expression is used by the Lord Jesus in
the Sermon on the Mount when He said 'You have heard
that it was said, "You shall not commit adultery". But I say
to you that everyone who looks at a woman lustfully has
already committed adultery with her in his heart' (Matthew
5:27–28 RSV). The thought is as guilty as the deed; in fact,
it is the parent of it. That being so, we ought to stay here
for a moment longer. It has been said that a man is not
what he thinks he is; but what he thinks, he is. That being
so, it is vitally important that our minds should be fed and
filled with the right material. How many troubles and even
disasters have begun and gathered momentum in the mind,
especially a mind that is lazy, undisciplined, unguarded!
The biblical defence against that kind of situation is clear,
particularly in the following two passages. Writing to the
Colossians, Paul says 'If then you have been raised with
Christ, seek the things that are above, where Christ is, seated
at the right hand of God. Set your minds on things that are
above, not on things that are on earth' (Colossians 3:1–2
RSV); while in his letter to the Philippians he says 'Finally,
brethren, whatever is true, whatever is honourable, whatever
is just, whatever is pure, whatever is lovely, whatever is
gracious; if there is any excellence, if there is anything
worthy of praise, think about these things' (Philippians 4:8
RSV). In that second verse, the Amplified Bible adds the
phrase 'fix your minds on them', and perhaps that helps to
hammer home the practical discipline built into Paul's
words. In our sophisticated 20th Century we have not
altogether lost the art of study. In fact a great deal of study

is necessary today to obtain technical qualifications. But I wonder if we have lost the deeper art of *meditation?* Only as the mind is filled with the fruits both of study of the biblical facts and meditation on biblical truths will the springs of the mind and the desires be kept clean. So much for the two phrases 'Ye lust' and '(ye) desire to have'.

Secondly – we have the two phrases 'have not' and 'cannot obtain'. It is one thing to want something, but it is quite another thing to obtain it; nobody can disagree with that! James is to give a reason for this later, but just for the moment he states the simple pathetic fact that desire does not equal achievement, or, to be even more blunt, sin does not equal satisfaction. Remember that he is speaking primarily about evil desires, about putting self before God, and the point he is driving home here is that we can put self first as long as we like, but it still does not produce satisfaction. 'Satisfaction' is a much longer word than 'self', and satisfaction is a much bigger thing than wanting that which would please us. Dr Samuel Johnson, the famous 18th Century man of letters, once said, 'Of all that have tried the selfish experiment, let one come forth and say that he has succeeded. He that has made gold his idol, has it satisfied him? He that has toiled in the fields of ambition, has he been repaid? He that has ransacked every theatre of sensual enjoyment, is he content? Can any answer in the affirmative? Not one!' As John Macmurray succinctly put it, 'The best cure for hedonism is the attempt to practice it'!

Yet no comment on this issue is more devastating than the Bible's own words. Read carefully these words by an Old Testament preacher – 'I said to myself, "Come now, I will make a test of pleasure; enjoy yourself". But behold, this also was vanity. I said of laughter, "It is mad", and of pleasure, "What use is it?" I searched with my mind how to cheer my body with wine – my mind still guiding me with wisdom – and how to lay hold on folly, till I might see what was good for the sons of men to do under heaven during the few days of their life. I made great works; I built houses and planted vineyards for myself; I made myself gardens and parks, and planted in them all kinds of fruit trees. I bought male and female slaves, and had slaves who were born in my house; I had also great possessions of herds and flocks, more than any who had been before me in Jerusalem. I also gathered for myself silver and gold and the treasure of kings and provinces; I got singers, both men and women, and many concubines, man's delight. So I became great and surpassed all who were before me in Jerusalem; also my wisdom remained with me. And whatever my eyes desired I did not keep from them; I kept my heart from no pleasure, for my heart found pleasure in all my toil, and this was my reward for all my toil'. (Ecclesiastes 2: 1-10 RSV).

In those ten verses, the words 'I', 'my' and 'myself' occur over 30 times. It is a passage motivated entirely by the desire to have. Yet when all this storm of desire is over, what do we discover? This is the wording of the very next verse – 'Then I considered all that my hands had done and the toil I had spent in doing it, and behold, all was vanity, and a striving after wind, and there was nothing to be gained under the sun'. (Ecclesiastes 2: 11 RSV).

Thirdly, we come to the third group of phrases that James uses, what I have called the 'climax' words – 'ye kill' and 'ye fight and war'. Bear in mind the progression of thought here. James speaks first of all of thoughts and desires in the heart; then of discovering that the more these are selfishly pursued the more dissatisfaction they bring; now he says that this situation breaks out into murder, into fighting and war. Is he overstating the case? His language is certainly strong, but James had history on his side, and his readers would remember at least two famous Old Testament stories of people who desired, could not obtain, and so killed until they got what they wanted. The first classic case is told in 2 Samuel 11, the story of David, Bathsheba and Uriah the Hittite. The other is in 1 Kings 21, the story of the rich king Ahab, the wicked Jezebel, and the innocent Naboth who was eventually killed in order that Ahab could add his one small vineyard to his other possessions. Never underestimate the tremendous power of human desire. It is surely obvious that Adam must have been created with a tremendously strong desire, one that kept him utterly pure and obedient to the will of God, perhaps for a very long time. Now that he is fallen, man finds that that desire is twisted, warped,

perverted but it is still almost unbelievably strong. It seeks
to rip aside everything and anything that stands in its way.
Unfulfilled desire produces tension, strife, hasty decisions,
irrational actions, and even goes as far as murder. The word
'kill' used by James could be translated 'destroy', which
quickly reminds us that according to the Bible a word is
just as effective as a knife, a thought is just as devastating
as a gun, and a criticism can be just as serious and corroding
as poison. This is how the Apostle John put it – 'Any one
who hates his brother is a murderer' (1 John 3:15 RSV),
while Jesus said, 'You have heard that it was said to the
men of old, "You shall not kill; and whosoever kills shall
be liable to judgment". But I say to you that everyone who
is angry with his brother shall be liable to judgment; whoever
insults his brother shall be liable to the council, and whoever
says "You fool!" shall be liable to the hell of fire' (Matthew
5:21–22 RSV).

Make no mistake about it – character, reputation, the
progress of Christian work, the prospect of a special effort,
harmony in the home – all of these things can be destroyed,
killed, because of our desire to put self first. This is the
climax James reaches in this part of his letter. He shows his
readers that their passions were destructive. So are ours! –
and we must therefore seek to ensure that they are consecra-
ted to the Lord, that we are mastered by one desire only,
and that is the desire to do His will.

Now we can move on to the second thing that James is
telling his readers. Not only were their passions destructive,
but

2. *THEIR PRAYER WAS DEFECTIVE* – '. . . yet ye
have not, because ye ask not. Ye ask, and receive not,
because ye ask amiss, that ye may consume it upon your
lusts'. (verses 2b–3).

There is something quite devastating in the way James
writes here. He is brief, blunt, but utterly realistic. In a
phrase, he is saying that their prayer was defective, but he
puts this one statement in four ways. He begins by saying
that their prayer was defective –

(1) *In its content* – 'ye have not, because ye ask not'. In
plain language, one reason they did not obtain certain things

was that they did not pray for them. Their prayer was defective in its content because its content was nil! Of course there may have been a simple reason why they did not pray for certain things, namely that they knew perfectly well that they could not honestly do so. The things they wanted were things about which it would have been useless to pray. The things they wanted were wrong, or their desire to have them was wrong. There is a simple but clear principle here: if you cannot pray about it, then you will not profit from it. That principle can be written across the whole of life, across every situation, whether we are young, or old, or in the middle of life. If we cannot pray about it, then we cannot profit from it. If we cannot say, 'Lord, bless me as I do this thing', we ought not to be doing it at all. Of course, all prayerlessness in effect leads to fealure in obtaining, as Joseph Scriven wrote in his famous hymn:—

> O what peace we often forfeit,
> O what needless pain we bear,
> All because we do not carry
> Everything to God in prayer!

Is there any measure in which that can be said of you? Is your prayer defective in its content? Are there whole tracts of your life about which you never pray? Are there issues which you never take to the throne of grace? Is it therefore surprising that you are disappointed in those very same areas, and that things do not seem to work out? Of how many good, legitimate, godly things, of how many blessings for yourself and other people could it be said, 'you have not because you ask not'? Then James goes on to say that their prayer was defective —

(2) *In its consequence* — 'Ye ask, and receive not'. Have you noticed that pathetic refrain in these two verses? — '(Ye) have not', '(ye) cannot obtain', 'ye have not', '(ye) receive not'. These verses are marked not only by intense desire, but by immense disappointment. In verse 2, in fact, 'obtain' has as its root a word meaning 'to hit the mark', 'to attain', 'to reach one's end', or 'to be successful' — and all of these things are missing!

Two little phrases in the story of the Prodigal Son bring

this sense of unfulfilment out dramatically. In the early part of the story his whole attitude can be summed up in two words – 'give me' (Luke 15:12), but before long he is described in two vastly different words – 'in want'. There are the same two elements – intense desire and immense disappointment. He got what he wanted, but it was not what he needed. It failed to satisfy. Here, surely, is a lesson that we must never stop learning, that just as a triangle will never fill a circle, so the world can never fill and satisfy a man's deepest needs. It can meet some of those needs, at a certain level, for a certain time, and in a certain way, but the world cannot fill a man's total needs.

Matthew Henry once said 'It should kill these lusts to think of their disappointment', but man is in some ways a fatal optimist and he just goes on hoping and trying and scheming and striving. Surely there is no clearer evidence of the presence and the persistence of indwelling sin, than the futile and fatal pursuit of that which cannot satisfy! Listen to the patient appeal of God's word 'Why do you spend your money for that which is not bread? and your labour for that which does not satisfy?' (Isaiah 55:2 RSV). There are times when God's sternest rebuke is to give us the things we ask for, so that we see that they do not satisfy us; and there are times when His greatest love is shown in His refusal to give us those things that we want. Now notice how James develops his argument by showing that their prayer was defective –

(3) *In its conception.* '. . . because ye ask amiss'. It may be that there is no phrase in the whole of the epistle of James that has wounded me more often than this particular one – 'because ye ask amiss'. This is one of the reasons for what we call 'unanswered prayer. The RSV translates the phrase 'you ask wrongly'; literally the Greek means, 'you ask out of place'; Matthew Henry's pithy comment is 'We miss when we ask amiss'. It is not so much a matter of asking for the wrong things, as of asking in the wrong way. Let me illustrate from the story of the Pharisee and the Publican told in Luke 18. Jesus never condemned the Pharisee because of the things he did – his tithing, his generosity, the fact that he was a contented man, his moral purity and so on. He was

condemned because he gave them the wrong value. Again, in verse 18 of chapter 3, James says the work of peace-making has to be done in the right spirit. It is the attitude, the approach, the motive that makes so much difference here. We must remember that there are clear conditions for answered prayer, and the over-ruling one is this – 'And this is the confidence which we have in Him, that if we ask anything according to His will He hears us' (1 John 5 : 14 RSV). Notice the crucial phrase! It is not just a matter of asking, but of asking *according to God's will*. Does that not search and humble us as we examine our prayer lives?

I once heard Alec Motyer put it like this: 'If it were the case that whatever we ask, God was pledged to give, then I for one would never pray again, because I would not have sufficient confidence in my own wisdom to ask God for anything!'

The fact is that we need to be as dependent upon God for our prayers as we are for His answers. Paul says quite clearly 'we do not know how to pray as we ought' (Romans 8 : 26 RSV). We just do not have this wisdom in us by nature. We need the wisdom of the Holy Spirit in order to pray aright. Prayer is not just a concoction of words that we say with our knees bent and our eyes closed. We need more than bent knees and closed eyes. We need an open, broken, humble, dependent, thirsting, believing heart. And we need the desire that in our prayer God's will shall come first. Otherwise we shall 'ask amiss'. Before we pass on, just notice a few other scriptures that teach quite clearly that there is no automatic answer to our prayers. 'There they cry out, but He does not answer, because of the pride of evil men. Surely God does not hear an empty cry, nor does the Almighty regard it' (Job 35 : 12–13 RSV); 'When you spread forth your hands, I will hide my eyes from you; even though you make many prayers, I will not listen; your hands are full of blood' (Isaiah 1 : 15 RSV); 'Then they will cry to the Lord, but He will not answer them; He will hide His face from them at that time, because they have made their deeds evil' (Micah 3 : 4 RSV); 'If I regard iniquity in my heart, the Lord will not hear me' (Psalm 66 : 18).

These verses all underline the negative side of a clear

biblical principle, yet we must not press the point so logically
that we think that we can earn ourselves the right to be
answered because of our obedience. Let us be careful here.
It is certainly true that we cannot get the gratification of evil,
wrongly motivated desire, just by praying for it. But we
cannot press the reverse so far that we believe in God answering our prayer because our obedience has earned us the right
to be answered. We have been examining God's law, written
for our learning, but we must place it alongside God's love,
and when we do that we discover that when God answers our
smallest prayer, at our finest moment, then He only does so
by overwhelming our unworthiness with His incomprehen-
sible grace. Every answer to prayer is an answer of grace,
and not of reward or merit. It is God overwhelming our
unworthiness with His grace. And if that does not make
sense, it is because God's ways are higher than our ways. It
may not pacify the logical mind, but it satisfies the longing
heart!

So far James has shown his readers' prayer to be defective in its content, its consequence and its conception. He
now adds one last thing; he says it is defective –

(4) *In its concern* – 'that ye may consume it upon your
lusts'. The word 'lusts' here, is, as in verse 1, the word
'*hedonon*', the pleasure derived from the fulfilment of desire.
The point here shifts from *how* they prayed to *why* they
prayed. The Amplified Bible says 'you ask with wrong purpose and evil, selfish motives. Your intention is, when you
get what you desire, to spend it in sensual pleasures'. This
unmasks the real concern of their prayer – it was entirely
selfish. It is said that the following prayer was found among
the papers of John Ward, a Member of Parliament who
owned part of Dagenham.

'O Lord, thou knowest that I have mine estates in the City
of London, and likewise that I have lately purchased an
estate in the county of Essex. I beseech thee to preserve the
two counties of Middlesex and Essex from fire and earth-
quake; and as I have a mortgage in Hertfordshire, I beg of
thee likewise to have an eye of compassion on that county.
As for the rest of the counties, thou mayest deal with them
as thou art pleased'.

No doubt the inhabitants of the counties concerned would have been grateful if they had known of his prayers! – but his concern was not for them, but for himself. His motive was wrong.

It is possible to pray for many good things in the wrong way. For instance, it is possible to pray for the conversion of one's parents or children primarily because it would be so much better to live in a Christian home. It is possible to pray for the conversion of a workmate because he is a difficult fellow with whom to work and it would be marvellous if he were converted. It is possible to pray for a missionary need to be met in order to avoid the pressure of the need. It is possible to pray for the success of your church, your fellowship, your Christian work or organisation because that would increase its stature. What is *your* concern when you pray? When you pray for those missionaries, when you pray for your church, when you pray for your home, your parents, your children, what is your concern? What is the *first* concern? What could you write above your prayer time that would sum up exactly the primary concern of your intercession? Incidentally, there is a link between concern and consequence, in that the word 'consume' that James uses here, is the same word that is used in Luke 15, when we are told that the Prodigal Son '*spent* all and began to be in want', and of the woman in Mark 5 who had been ill for twelve years and who, despite numerous visits to doctors, had '*spent* all that she had and was nothing better'. Is there not something significant in the use of that very word by James? – it indicates yet again the terrible emptiness which follows selfish praying. God's promise is to supply our need, not our greed. Prayer is not asking God for what we want, it is asking God for what *He* wants!

Man's ruin began in the Garden of Eden, when in spirit the first Adam said 'Not Thy will but mine be done'. Man's rescue came towards its consummation when in another garden the second Adam said 'Not my will, but Thine, be done' (Luke 24:42). That is the spirit that should characterise all of our praying. That should be our one dominating concern. If there is one thing above all that will prevent a prayer from being defective, it is that when we fall on our knees to pray we should have a single eye to the glory of God; regardless of what it might cost us; regardless of what plans of ours might go astray; regardless of whether our particular church, or fellowship, or group, or missionary society thrives and flourishes or is pushed on one side for another work of God to come in. When we pray like that, then our prayer will be effective, God will be glorified, His Kingdom will be extended, and we will be truly blessed.

Chapter 3

BACKSLIDING UNMASKED

'Ye adulterers and adulteresses, know ye not that the friendship of the world is enmity with God? whosoever therefore will be a friend of the world is the enemy of God.

Do ye think that the scripture saith in vain, The spirit that dwelleth in us lusteth to envy?' (James 4:4-5)

In our previous two studies, we have seen James at work in exposing the root causes of strife and unrest in the world at large, in communities, in churches, and in the hearts of individual Christians. These were all seen to be part of man's fallen nature, still actively at work, and one result was to make a man's prayer life defective. In other words, they drew a man away from a settled, happy relationship with the Lord.

It is this matter of relationship that James now takes up in verses 4-5. Two general headings will help us to gather together the impact of his words.

1. *THEIR CONDUCT IS EXPOSED* – 'Ye adulterers and adulteresses, know ye not that the friendship of the world is enmity with God? whosoever therefore will be a friend of the world is the enemy of God' (verse 4).

Remember that James is writing to Christian people, but it is obvious from the forcefulness of his language here that at this point he is writing to believers who are backsliders. They are people who, in their thinking, their acting, their speaking, their attitudes, their approach to life, their scheming, their envying and selfish ambition, are betraying their faith, deserting their Lord and resorting to earthly wisdom. That, I think, is not too harsh a summary of what James has been saying. Towards the end of chapter 3 he showed the difference between spiritual, godly, heavenly wisdom, and the false wisdom of the world, with the clear inference that Christians who employ earthly wisdom are in fact back-

sliders. They are deserting their Lord and resorting to attitudes and actions that are 'earthly, sensual, devilish' (3:15).
In the verse now before us James rips aside all the rational-
ism that men use to defend their actions, all the excuses
these people make, and he exposes their backsliding for
what it really is. He gives it three descriptions, each one of
which is vivid in its language and deeply challenging in its
implications. Let us look at the three things James says about
backsliding.

(1) *It is adultery* – 'Ye adulterers and adulteresses' (v. 4a)
or, as the Revised Standard Version puts it 'Unfaithful
creatures!' The first point to make here is that there is not
necessarily any suggestion whatever of the physical sin of
adultery having been committed. Some older manuscripts
omit the phrase 'adulterers and', and it may well be that in
the original, all that James wrote was the single phrase translated 'you adulteresses'. Men and women were all joined
together under this one crashing condemnation. If they were
backsliding, if they were out of step with the Lord, if they
were deliberately pursuing earthly wisdom, instead of seeking, receiving and exercising spiritual grace and heavenly
wisdom, then they were adulteresses. Now why are male and
female joined together under the one feminine description
of 'adulteresses'? To get the answer to that we have to go
back to the Old Testament and to one of the most wonderful pictures the Bible gives us of God's relationship to His
people. Here are three of the places where we find it used:–
'For your Maker is your husband, the Lord of hosts is His
name' (Isaiah 54:5 RSV); 'Turn, O backsliding children,
saith the Lord; for I am married unto you' (Jeremiah 3:14);
'Surely, as a faithless wife leaves her husband, so have you
been faithless to me, O house of Israel, says the Lord'
(Jeremiah 3:20 RSV). The picture we have in these verses
is the lovely one of the Lord as the Husband of His people;
His people as the wife of their Lord and Master. But we see
this not only in the Old Testament and concerning the old
Israel, but in the New Testament, concerning the new,
spiritual Israel, comprised of all believers in the Lord Jesus.
The Apostle Paul writes, 'Wherefore, my brethren, ye also
are become dead to the law by the body of Christ; that ye

should be married to another, even to Him who is raised from the dead, that we should bring forth fruit unto God' (Romans 7:4); and again, 'I feel a divine jealousy for you, for I betrothed you to Christ to present you as a pure bride to her one husband' (2 Corinthians 11:2 RSV); and again, in that lovely word to the Ephesians, 'Therefore as the church is subject unto Christ, so let the wives be to their own husbands in everything. Husbands, love your wives, even as Christ also loved the church, and gave himself for it; that he might sanctify and cleanse it with the washing of water by the word, that he might present it to himself a glorious church, not having spot, or wrinkle, or any such thing; but that it should be holy and without blemish' (Ephesians 5:24–27). The Apostle John gives us the same picture as he records the voice of a great multitude in heaven crying 'Let us be glad and rejoice, and give honour to him: for the marriage of the Lamb is come, and his wife hath made herself ready' (Revelation 19:7).

The Bible is wonderfully rich in the total imagery that it uses to describe the relationship between Christ and the Christian, while those untaught in the scriptures tend to be so narrow in their appreciation of our relationship to the Lord. Someone only recently converted, for instance, might think merely in terms of the fact that Jesus is their Saviour. All of their thoughts would be centred around His substitutionary death for them on the cross. Perhaps their emphasis would be mainly on the fact that their sins were forgiven and that Jesus had forgiven them. We might almost say that their prime thoughts of Him might be as their Forgiver, rather than their Saviour. Then their understanding of the word 'Saviour' would begin to grow, and they would learn to appreciate that He had saved them not only from the past, but from the present and the future too, in terms of the power of sin to keep them from God. From there, they would broaden out to ever widening appreciation of what the Bible says about their eternal relationship to Christ; but nowhere would they discover a more wonderful picture than this – the Bridegroom and the Bride! In the marriage service in the Book of Common Prayer, the bride is asked whether she will 'forsaking all other, keep thee only unto him as long as ye both shall live', to which she is required to answer 'I will'. Here is the solemn vow that lies at the heart of holy matrimony. And when that vow is broken, we say that adultery has been committed. Whether it is once or often, whether it is discovered or not, regardless of whether there are extenuating circumstances, the fact of the matter is that with that sin, the relationship is fractured. Now in drawing a spiritual analogy, let us be very careful to guard against saying three things. Firstly, that a person becomes a Christian by making a vow to God, by making a promise to the Lord Jesus Christ. Nobody becomes a Christian by making promises to God. Secondly, that one remains a Christian by *keeping* promises to God. That would remove salvation from the realm of grace altogether. Thirdly, we must guard against saying that one sin or, indeed, many sins put a Christian outside of God's family, in other words that a man can sin away his salvation. Let us not make any of those three mistakes, but let none of our carefulness in avoding those errors allow us to escape the impact of the point that James is making here, which is that worldliness, or backsliding, is spiritual adultery. It is loving something or someone else more than your rightful husband, the Lord Himself. The Amplified Bible translates the phrase, 'You are like unfaithful wives having illicit love affairs with the world and breaking your marriage vows to God!'

I remember a young man coming up to me during a youth Crusade I was conducting in the West Country and saying, 'I shall never be the same again after tonight. Up to now, I have been flirting with the world'. Here was a young man who had claimed that although he was a Christian, part of the Bride of the Lord Jesus, he had been flirting, carrying on an illicit affair by the general drift of his life. Have you ever given much thought to those two penetrating questions asked by Elihu? - 'If you have sinned, what do you accomplish against Him? And if your transgressions are multiplied, what do you do to Him?' (Job 35:6 RSV). If you sin, what do you do against God, against the Lord Jesus Christ, against your spiritual Husband? The answer is here in the Epistle of James – you break His heart, because you break your vow. You commit spiritual adultery. The backslider is an adulteress. He has broken his vow to the Lord. Backsliding is adultery.

(2) *It is antagonism* – 'Know ye not that the friendship of the world is enmity with God? Whosoever therefore will be a friend of the world is the enemy of God' (v. 4b).

One of the most terrible things the Bible says about unconverted people is that they cannot please God. As the Apostle Paul puts it, 'For the mind that is set on the flesh is hostile to God; it does not submit to God's law, indeed it cannot; and those who are in the flesh *cannot please God*' (Romans 8 : 7–8 RSV). Unbelievers can please themselves, they can please the world, they can please the church, have a life of social acceptability, but what they cannot do is to please God, and the reason they cannot please God is that their whole minds are 'hostile to God'. The unbeliever's mind is carnal, it is not spiritually enlightened, directed or controlled. And we were once like that! Paul reminds the Christians at Colosse that they were once 'enemies in your mind by wicked works' (Colossians 1 : 21) – yet in God's amazing grace, that enmity of ours, that deep rooted Adamic enmity with which we were born and which developed as we grew up, was overwhelmed in the saving death of the Lord Jesus; '. . . when we were enemies, we were reconciled to God by the death of His Son. . . .' (Romans 5 : 10). Notice the precise wording here. It does not say that, though we were once God's enemies, we brought ourselves to a better frame of mind and decided to reconcile ourselves. It was '*when* we were enemies' that we were reconciled. It was while we were still pursuing a course that was dead set against God, the Cross, and the blood of the Lamb, a course that was utterly earthly and carnal in its whole essence – it was *then* that God reconciled us to Himself in the death of His Son. In the words of the hymnwriter,

> *Dear Lord, what heavenly wonders dwell*
> *In Thy atoning blood!*
> *By this are sinners snatched from hell,*
> *And rebels brought to God!*

Against that background of understanding, surely James is saying this: that backsliding or worldliness is going back in spirit to what we were before we were converted. It is going back to the place where we were antagonistic to God. It is standing at Calvary uncommitted to Christ, fingering the nails, twisting the crown of thorns, handling the spear, passing a hammer to the Roman soldier. That is what world-liness is. It is antagonism. Is that language too strong? Not according to the Apostle John, who said 'Do not love the world or the things in the world. If any one loves the world, love for the Father is not in him' (1 John 2:15 RSV). Not according to Paul, who speaks of those who are 'Traitors, heady, highminded, lovers of pleasure more than lovers of God' (2 Timothy 3:4). Not according to Jesus, who said 'No man can serve two masters; for either he will hate the one, and love the other, or he will be devoted to the one and despise the other. You cannot serve God and mammon' (Matthew 6:24 RSV). Not according to the Apostle James, who says here 'know ye not that the friendship of the world is enmity with God? Whosoever therefore will be a friend of the world is the enemy of God'. Notice, by the way, the little phrase, 'whosoever will be'. The Revised Standard Version translates it 'whoever wishes to be'. Outward action is not necessary. We do not have to be worldly in action in order to be guilty of worldliness. The wish alone is enough to find us guilty. If we are longing to break out of what seems to be our Christian straight-jacket and do something that the world is doing; if we envy what the world is having; then that is worldliness, and worldliness is antagonism. We must make up our minds, not only conclusively but continually, whether we are hungering to be transformed or whether we are happy to be conformed.

In his book 'Blessings out of Buffetings', Dr Alan Redpath says 'It is sheer, downright sin . . . for one generation, for the sake of its worldly convenience, to imagine that it can lower the bars of separation which are rooted in divine history, and revealed in divine prophecy, when we live in a world that is under God's judgment, and doomed to destruction, and when Jesus Christ is returning to take his people home'.

If you were to ask a young Christian 'Why did Jesus die?' he would probably centre his answer around the fact that Jesus died to forgive his sins. Indeed, many people outside of the church, if asked why Jesus died, would use phrases that referred, however vaguely, with sins being forgiven and put out of the way. But that by no means exhausts what the Bible says about the death of the Lord Jesus. Let us not forget that 'to this end Christ died and lived again that he might be *Lord* . . .' (Romans 14:9 RSV), and when we deny His rightful lordship in our lives, we are guilty of antagonism.

Not only is backsliding unmasked as adultery and antagonism –

(3) *It is audacity.* Where do I discover that? Well, I believe we have it at the beginning of verse 5 – 'Do ye think that the scripture saith in vain?' In the Authorised Version there is a comma at that point, and then the verse goes on to say 'The spirit that dwelleth in us lusteth to envy?' but I am going to be arbitrary here and say that I prefer a full-stop after the word 'vain'. Most people take this phrase exactly as it is in the Authorised Version, in which case it refers to what follows, and the whole verse runs through as one piece – 'Do ye think that the scripture saith in vain, The spirit that dwelleth in us lusteth to envy?' That may well be so, but I suggest it is just possible that the phrase refers to what came *before.* In this case the whole phrase would read like this – 'Ye adulterers and adulteresses, know ye not that the friendship of the world is enmity with God? Whosoever therefore will be a friend of the world is the enemy of God. Do ye think that the scriptures saith in vain?' The force of the last phrase would then be this – 'Do you think that the scriptures speak in an empty way, when they speak about spiritual adultery and enmity against God?' (Incidentally, the point as to whether the phrase applies to verse 4 or the second part of verse 5 does not affect the application in any way, because in point of fact neither verse 4 nor the second part of verse 5 appear in the Old Testament scriptures at all. In using the phrase, James is not introducing a specific verse of scripture. What he is saying is that the spirit of his words appears throughout scripture, and he assumed that his readers would know this perfectly well. Paul uses the same formula when he writes ' "Therefore" it is said "Awake O sleeper, and arise from the dead, and Christ shall give you light" '

(Ephesians 5:14 RSV). In fact, we have no scripture that says that, although the scriptures breath its spirit again and again. That seems to be the sort of formula that James is using).

Now I have chosen the word 'audacity' here because I feel there may be an important link between the two phrases 'know ye not' in verse 4, (perhaps inferring that they *do* know) and the phrase, 'Do ye think that the scripture saith in vain?' in verse 5. They *knew* what the scriptures said, and James's withering criticism was that they were deliberately and consistently taking a chance on God's grace and goodness. Or perhaps they were rationalising their behaviour to line it up with the world; or they were escaping behind some form of dispensationalism, or some loose interpretation. Worse still, perhaps they were deliberately letting the Word of God go no further than their heads. If James is moving along any of those lines then the lesson to us is this: let us beware of any kind of approach to scripture that is nothing short of sheer audacity. Let us never be guilty of reading the Word, understanding what it says, and then deliberately giving it less than the full obedience that it demands. That is audacity! Do you think the scripture speaks in vain? Do you think that the Bible is just a collection of empty words? That is sheer audacity! It is sheer audacity to come to the scriptures, read them, understand them, and then go and live as though they had not spoken at all. All scripture is valid, all of its promises are true and all of its warnings are real.

Here, then, is the backslider unmasked, in his adultery, sinning against love; his antagonism, sinning against law; and his audacity, sinning against the light. Now to the final phrase in this section, in which

2. *A CHALLENGE IS EXTENDED* – 'The spirit that dwelleth in us lusteth to envy'.

If you ask where the challenge is in this phrase, then the first answer is that it is a challenge to anyone who attempts to explain it! – because it is a candidate for the title of the most difficult verse in the whole Epistle. As long ago as the 16th Century, the Dutch humanist Desiderius Erasmus, who prepared a complete text of the New Testament, said 'There

are wagon-loads of interpretations of this passage'! Almost
every word has been under fire and they have been permu-
tated in almost every conceivable order. Let me illustrate its
difficulties. In studying the word 'spirit', I looked at 18 translations, and discovered that nine of them take the word to
mean the Holy Spirit, six take it to refer to the spirit of man,
that is his human nature, and three of them were completely
ambiguous as to what they meant! When I had finished
examining all the technicalities of the verse I could only pray
'Lord, what wilt thou have me to do'! I think the most helpful thing to do will be to look at three translations, covering
what seem to be the most likely possible areas of James's
meaning. In each case – though in very different ways – a
challenge is extended.

(1) *The New English Bible*. – 'The spirit which God implanted in man turns to envious desires'. Here the words
'lusteth' and 'envy' in the Authorised Version are combined
to be given a bad meaning. If this was James's intention, then
perhaps he was taking up the phrase in verse 1, 'your lusts
that war in your members'. If so, the challenge here is the
challenge to face up to the sobering reality of the residual
impact of our fallen nature – the spirit which God implanted
in man, originally good, but corrupted by the fall, is still,
even after conversion, liable to break out into 'envious
desires'. I remember reading with great interest the story of
Dr Christian Barnard, the first man in the world to perform
a heart transplant operation. On one occasion, he was talking to one of his transplant patients, Dr Philip Blaiberg, and
suddenly asked 'Would you like to see your old heart?'
Blaiberg said that he would. At 8 o'clock one evening the
two men stood in a room of the Groote Schuur Hospital, in
Johannesburg, South Africa. Dr Barnard went up to a cup-
board, took down a glass container and handed it to Dr
Blaiberg. Inside that container was Blaiberg's old heart. For
a moment he stood there stunned into silence – the first man
in history ever to hold his own heart in his hands. Finally,
he broke the silence, and for ten minutes he plied Dr Barnard
with technical questions (Blaiberg himself was a dentist).
Then he turned to take a final look at the contents of the
glass container, and said 'So this is my old heart, that caused

me so much trouble'. He handed it back, turned away, and left it for ever.

Now the point of that illustration is this: conversion is not a transplant. Conversion is not a taking away completely of our old heart and the implanting of a new one, so that we can look back and say, 'There was a day when I had an old heart, an old nature, that caused me so much trouble, but it can never cause me any trouble now because it has been permanently removed'. The verb 'lusteth' ('turns' in the NEB) is in the present continuous tense. The old nature, the old spirit, the old heart remains with us. We must face up to the continuing presence of our old nature.

(2) *The paraphrase by J. B. Phillips* – 'Do you imagine that this spirit of passionate jealousy is the Spirit He has caused to live in us?' Here, the words 'lusteth' and 'envy' are again combined to be given a bad meaning and what James is saying is something like this – 'Do you seriously think that the Holy Spirit who came to live within you at your conversion, is responsible for your passionate jealousy? Do you think that He is responsible for the kind of life you are living?' If that is the right interpretation, then James is taking up what he was saying in chapter 1, when he said, 'Let no man say when he is tempted, "I am tempted of God": for God cannot be tempted with evil, neither tempteth he any man' (v. 14). We cannot offload on to God the responsibility for our own failure. Although we can never obey God without His help, we can never blame God when we fail. Maybe what James is attacking is a kind of antinomianism – the doctrine that says, 'I am not under law, I am under grace, and the more I sin, the more grace will abound, and my sin will eventually result in the glory of God'. James completely destroys that argument here, and lays before us the challenge of our continuing personal responsibility to 'live godly in Christ Jesus' (2 Timothy 3:12).

(3) *The translation by Dr R. F. Weymouth* – 'The Spirit which He has caused to dwell in us yearns jealously over us'. Here is an entirely different interpretation. The words 'lusteth' and 'envy', are combined to be given a *good* sense. They are said to describe the activity of the Holy Spirit towards believers. This brings us face to face with one of the

most wonderful attributes of God, namely His jealousy. In
present day use, of course, 'jealousy' has a totally bad con-
notation, but it has a completely different meaning when the
Bible uses it about God. It is not the jealousy of selfish
possessiveness, nor of carnal desire, but of loving concern.

Let us just note some references. In the Ten Commandments we read – 'I the Lord your God am a jealous God'
(Exodus 20:5 RSV). Later, the Lord says to Moses '. . . for
you shall worship no other god, for the Lord, whose name is
Jealous, is a jealous God' (Exodus 34:14 RSV). God says
to Zechariah 'I am jealous for Zion with great jealousy, and
I am jealous for her with great wrath' (Zechariah 8:2 RSV).

In closing this study, let us mark three things about this
Divine jealousy –

Firstly, it is an intense jealousy – 'I am jealous for Zion
with *great* jealousy', says God. In the book from which I
quoted earlier, Alan Redpath says 'The jealousy of God
. . . is the greatest flame that burns in the heart of deity . . .
a concern for the purity, the holiness, the greatness, the glory
of his people'. What a marvellous, humbling thing, that God
has an intense jealousy that we should be a pure, holy, great
and glorious people!

Secondly, it is an infinite jealousy. It is an attribute of God,
and therefore it is an eternal and infinite thing. It is not
something acquired, it is not something developed, it is not
something prompted by circumstances, it is not something
suggested by anything that we are, or anything that we have,
or anything that we become, or any obedience that we render,
or any sacrifice we make, or any faith we exercise. Are you
a Christian? Then let me apply this to you personally. It is
the jealousy of the Divine Lover of His people, the One Who
loves you with an everlasting love; Who was jealous for you
the moment you first drew breath upon this earth; Who was
jealous for you when you were groping for the first hold on
life; Who was jealous for your holiness and your salvation,
when you were beginning to learn the ways of the world;
Who was jealous for you when you took those first conscious steps into sin; jealous for you when you first heard His
Name; jealous for you when you rejected Him; jealous for
your salvation as He brought the gospel to you in one way

or another, through one person or another, through one means or another, until finally He broke through in the power of the Holy Spirit. And, He is jealous for you now, and for your spiritual welfare, in every temptation and under every pressure, jealous lest you should be robbed by Satan, or by sin, or by stupidity, or by covetousness, or compromise, or worldliness, or lack of prayer or disobedience in any shape or form. He is jealous that you should have that fullness of blessing, those riches of grace that He longs to bestow upon every one of His people. When we speak about the Jealous God, we mean at least all of that, for this jealousy is an infinite jealousy.

Thirdly, it is an intimate jealousy – The Holy Spirit dwells '*in* us'. This Divine jealousy is not exercised by God in some remote kind of way, distantly and outwardly and objectively and externally – but by the Holy Spirit Himself dwelling within the heart of every believer.

Harriet Auber put it like this in one of her hymns –

> *And His that gentle voice we hear,*
> *Soft as the voice of even;*
> *That checks each fault, and calms each fear,*
> *And speaks of Heaven.*

I said that this phrase was a challenge – and surely it is! If it is interpreted in the first way, it is a challenge that we still have to deal with the indwelling old nature. If the second interpretation is right, then the challenge is that we still have a personal responsibility to walk with the Lord day by day. If the third interpretation is correct, then we are asked to meditate on the glorious truth that the Holy Spirit, Who dwells within us, has a longing, yearning, jealousy that we should walk in the paths of godliness, safety and blessing day by day. Does that not challenge divided loyalty, and even the smallest backsliding?

Chapter 4

AMAZING GRACE!

'But he giveth more grace. Wherefore he saith, God resisteth the proud, but giveth grace unto the humble.'
(James 4:6)

In his book 'Grace in the New Testament', Dr James Moffatt makes this comment 'The religion of the Bible is a religion or grace or it is nothing . . . no grace, no gospel'. Surely every Christian will find it easy to agree with that statement! The mind runs quickly, for instance, to Paul's matchless verse, 'For by grace are ye saved through faith; and that not of yourselves: it is the gift of God: not of works, lest any man should boast' (Ephesians 2:8-9). Then there is his word to the elders at Ephesus about 'the gospel of the grace of God' (Acts 20:24). Peter, too, attributes our salvation entirely to 'the God of all grace' (1 Peter 5:10). Dr Moffatt is certainly right when he says 'No grace, no gospel'!

The verse before us now is a verse about grace, but before we begin to examine the text, we ought to take a close look at the general biblical use of the word. This will occupy the first part of our study, and the verse itself will occupy the second – but everything will centre around this one word – *grace!*

1. HOW IT IS GIVEN

As we read the Bible we discover that the grace of God comes to men in at least three ways. There is first of all –

(1) *Common grace.* 'A simple definition of grace would be 'undeserved favour', but this is by no means limited to its general evangelical contexts of salvation or those who are saved. David says 'The Lord is good to all and his tender mercies are over all his works' (Psalm 145:9), and later adds 'Thou openest thine hand, and satisfiest the desire of every living thing' (Psalm 145:16). Is that not obviously true? The smallest bird, the tiniest animal, the most microscopic fish, all of these have their needs met by their Creator. Certainly there is no difficulty in proving that all *men*, regardless of

their feelings about Him or their attitude towards Him, benefit from God's common grace, His undeserved favour to all men. The Apostle Paul says that God is 'the Saviour of all men, especially of those who believe' (1 Timothy 4:10 RSV). This is a most important verse in our understanding of what we have called 'common grace'. Notice that Paul says that God is the Saviour of 'all men'. What does he mean by that? It must be obvious that he does not mean that He is their Saviour in the evangelical sense of saving them from sin and giving them eternal life; because in the first place that would teach the unbiblical doctrine of universalism (that all men will eventually be saved) and in the second place it would render completely unnecessary Paul's next phrase 'especially of those who believe'. Then in what sense can we say that God is the Saviour of all men? If we were to take time to study the biblical development of the word 'Saviour', we would discover that some of its fundamental meanings include 'Preserver' and 'Deliverer', and if we apply Paul's words with those definitions in mind we come to a perfectly satisfying explanation. God *is* the Saviour of all men. Every moment that a man enjoys the benefits of a healthy body, God is saving him from illness; if a man is sane, God is saving him from a diseased mind; to whatever degree a man knows the truth about any subject whatever, God is saving him from error; when a man has food to eat and water to drink, God is saving him from starvation; every moment of good in a man's life is possible because God is saving him from the forces of evil; every thought, word and deed that has the slightest element of rightness about it is possible because God is at work saving that man from utter and complete corruption; in every moment of life, God is saving from death. As William Hendriksen says, 'He provides His creatures with food, keeps them alive, is deeply interested in them, often delivers them from disease, ills, hurt, famine, war, poverty, and peril in any form. He is, accordingly, their *Soter* (Preserver, Deliverer, and in *that* sense Saviour)'.

This is common grace, in the sense that God pours it out upon all men regardless of their faith or infidelity. As Jesus Himself put it, 'He makes His sun to rise on the evil and on

the good, and sends rain on the just and on the unjust'
(Matthew 5:45 RSV). God pours out this common grace
upon all men without distinction, upon the downright sinner
as well as upon the upright saint! To quote Hendriksen
again, 'There is no one who does not in one way or another
come within the reach of His benevolence'. From common
grace, let us move on to

(2) *Covenant grace*. This is what Paul means when he
speaks of 'this grace wherein we (as Christians) stand
(Romans 5:2). This has to do with God moving out to
redeem men lost in sin. It is especially and deliberately
identified with God's saving, redeeming acts. And it is not
an indiscriminate thing. It is individual and personal, in its
intention, application and acceptance. It is especially to
those who believe. It is interesting to notice that the first
time the word occurs in the Bible it is where we read that
'Noah found grace in the eyes of the Lord' (Genesis 6:8).
The immediate consequence, of course, was his physical
salvation, but the deeper truth is clear, and the whole context shows it to be a covenant word. It was so with Abraham,
and later with Isaac and with Jacob. Although the word
'grace' occurs very little in the Old Testament, its pages are
full of its meaning, the typical Old Testament words used
being 'mercy', 'kindness' and 'loving kindness'. The Old
Testament is full of covenant grace.

When we turn to the New Testament (or Covenant) we
come across something which at first glance is a tremendous
surprise, and that is that Jesus never once uses the word!
Yet He had no need to! His whole life was the grace of God
in salvation. As John put it, 'grace and truth came by Jesus
Christ' (John 1:17). This does not mean that there had been
no grace or truth before Jesus came, but that these things
were seen in their fullest form in the coming and the life of
Jesus. His whole coming into the world demonstrated the
grace of God. Paul writes to the Corinthian Christians 'For
you know the grace of our Lord Jesus Christ, that though
He was rich, yet for your sake He became poor, so that by
His poverty you might become rich' (2 Corinthians 8:9
RSV). Here we have wonderful blessing brought to the
wilfully bankrupt! The word 'grace' is a translation of the

Greek word *charis*, and it will help us to grasp its meaning in terms of salvation if we look at one very well known verse in which it is used. Writing to the Romans, Paul says, 'For the wages of sin is death; but the gift of God is eternal life through Jesus Christ our Lord' (Romans 6:23). Now the word 'gift' which Paul uses here is the Greek word *charisma*, which means a free unmerited gift. In other words, salvation is something on which man has no claim, and towards which he can make no contribution whatever. It is the free gift of God, something given entirely at His own will, moved by nothing except His own loving design. This is Paul's very clear argument in Romans 11 where he says 'So too at the present time there is a remnant, chosen by grace. But if it is by grace, it is no longer on the basis of works; otherwise grace would no longer be grace' (Romans 11:5–6 RSV). This underlines his word to the Ephesians that our salvation is 'by grace' and 'not of works'. The two things are mutually exclusive. The Christian's salvation is by covenant grace, free, unmerited, and unmixed in any way with human effort.

Few Christians have as dramatic a testimony as John Newton. A deserter, slave trader and infidel, the turning-point in his life came when he miraculously survived the terrifying Atlantic storm that struck the trading ship 'The Greyhound' in March 1748. After his conversion, he taught himself Greek and Hebrew, became a minister of the Gospel, and had a decisive influence on William Wilberforce, who was to lead the successful campaign for the abolition of the slave trade. John Newton also wrote a number of wonderful hymns, and one of the best-known gives poetic expression to so much of what the Bible says about covenant grace –

> *Amazing grace! (how sweet the sound!)*
> *That saved a wretch like me!*
> *I once was lost, but now am found;*
> *Was blind, but now I see.*
>
> *'Twas grace that taught my heart to fear,*
> *And grace my fears relieved;*
> *How precious did that grace appear,*
> *The hour I first believed!*

> Through many dangers, toils and snares,
> I have already come;
> 'Tis grace has brought me safe thus far,
> And grace will lead me home.
>
> The Lord has promised good to me,
> His word my hope secures:
> He will my shield and portion be,
> As long as life endures.
>
> Yes, when this flesh and heart shall fail,
> And mortal life shall cease;
> I shall possess, within the veil,
> A life of joy and peace.
>
> The earth shall soon dissolve like snow,
> The sun forbear to shine:
> But God, who called me here below,
> Will be for ever mine.

The words of Newton's hymn help us to link covenant grace to the third way in which the Bible uses the word –

(3) *Continuing grace.* This, I believe, is the particular sense in which James is using the word here. Not only is it God, and God alone, who can give the grace for a person to come to Christ; it is also true that God, and God alone, can give the grace for a person to continue in the Christian life. This is the first and only verse in which James uses this particular word. (The word translated 'grace' in chapter 1 verse 11 is an entirely different word).A very simple meaning of the word James uses here would be 'help', or 'strength' or 'spiritual power'. Although the verse now before us begins with the word 'But', it is a little difficult to establish an immediate link with the previous verse. Notice, however, how it may fit in with the possible alternative meanings of the latter part of verse 5, at which we looked in our previous study.

If we accept the first interpretation of that verse, then the link is one of contrast. While our human spirit, our old nature, still grasps enviously and jealously, the Holy Spirit is a Spirit of grace, of free giving. If the second interpretation is correct, then what James is saying is that far from the

Holy Spirit being responsible for our passionate jealousy and for leading us into sin, He pours in His continuing grace to help us to overcome these very things. If we accept the third interpretation, which tells us of God's intense, infinite and intimate yearning over our holiness, obedience and blessing, then He is adding this further verse to remind us that God gives the grace to carry out His demands. As Dr William Barclay has put it 'Only the grace of God can enable us to respond to the love of God'.

Whichever of those interpretations is correct, this remains certain, 'He giveth more grace'; and of that continual giving of grace we may say these two things: –

Firstly, it is according to His nature. The word 'giveth' is in the present continuous tense. It is a never-ending giving. The story is told of a man who submitted a painting to a well-known exhibition, but, by mistake, he forgot to give the painting a title. The work was an impression of the Niagara Falls, and showed the surging, seething waters pouring over the rocks. Just before the exhibition was due to open, the organiser noticed that it was without a title, and someone was given the responsibility of choosing one. After some thought he chose these three words – 'More to follow'. Do you see why? Those waters had poured over the rocks for countless years, bringing light, heat, comfort and many other benefits to multitudes of people – yet there was still more to follow, and multitudes more could be helped in the same way. The spiritual application is obvious. When we consider the grace of God, how wonderful it is to remember that although multitudes have drawn so hungrily and so continuously upon it for untold centuries, there is always more to follow. 'He giveth *more* grace'. It is given not only fully, and freely, but continuously – and that is completely according to the nature of 'the giving God' (James 1 : 5, The Amplified Bible).

Secondly, it is according to our need. The Amplified Bible has a wonderful elaboration of Hebrews 4 : 16. It translates it like this. 'Let us then fearlessly and confidently and boldly draw near to the throne of grace – the throne of God's unmerited favour to us sinners; that we may receive mercy for our failures and find grace to help in good time for every need – appropriate help and well-timed help coming just when we need it'. Just as there is never a time when we are without need, so there is never a time when we are without grace. In fact, we may say even more than that. Because God knows our every need in detail He is able to supply exactly the grace to meet its precise demands. For daily need there is daily grace. For sudden need there is sudden grace. For overwhelming need there is overwhelming grace. God's grace is given wonderfully but not wastefully; freely but not foolishly; bountifully but not blindly. Annie Johnson Flint has perfectly captured the spirit of this in these well known lines:

He giveth more grace when the burdens grow greater;
He sendeth more grace when the labours increase;
To added afflictions He addeth His mercy,
To multiplied trials His multiplied peace.

When we have exhausted our store of endurance,
When our strength has failed ere the day is half done:
When we reach the end of our hoarded resources,
Our Father's full giving is only begun.

His love has no limits, His grace has no measure,
His power has no boundary known unto men;
For out of His infinite riches in Jesus,
He giveth, and giveth, and giveth again.

So much for our brief study of how grace is given. Now let us turn to the text of our verse and notice
2. *HOW IT IS GOVERNED* – 'Wherefore he saith, God resisteth the proud, but giveth grace unto the humble'.

Let us first of all glance for a moment at the opening words – 'Wherefore he saith'. The word 'he' obviously refers to God, but the Revised Version translates the verse, 'Wherefore *the scripture* saith', and the Revised Standard Version has 'Therefore *it* says'. In essence, of course, all this amounts to the same thing! But which scripture says this? The general truth to which James is referring is taught many times in the scriptures but his words are the Septuagint Version (the earliest Greek translation of the Hebrew Old Testament) of a verse which reads like this in our Authorised Version –

'Surely he scorneth the scorners: but He giveth grace unto the humble' (Proverbs 3:34). Peter quotes this same verse in 1 Peter 5:5. It seems to me that these words are directions. They narrow the general down to the particular. They point us to the laws which apply in the matter of grace. Now this is not a contradiction! While grace is certainly not mechanical and automatic, yet it *is* governed by laws, and because those laws are Divine, they are perfectly consistent with the grace of God being free. God's mind is not in conflict with His heart.

Let us look at the two ways in which, according to this verse, the grace of God is governed.

(1) *The proud in spirit are resisted* – 'God resisteth the proud'.

This is one of the most terrible statements in the whole of the Bible, and all because of the meaning of the word 'resisteth'. There are four Greek words translated 'resist' in our Authorised Version. This one is the Greek word *antitasso*, which literally means 'to arrange against'. It is a military term. We could translate it 'to set in array as in a battle'. How wonderful to have the hosts of God encamped around you! – but just imagine what it must mean to have the God of hosts arranged against you! Yet James is saying nothing less than that in this verse. But why such strong language? Why such severe action? Because of the nature of pride! Because pride is the cause and core of so many other things. If we are right in assuming that Isaiah 14 tells us of Satan's fall from glory, then it was pride that joined with envy and ambition to bring it about, and hurled him from heaven. As Milton put it, 'Satan decided it was better to reign in hell than to serve in heaven'. In the Garden of Eden, Adam and Eve were lured by the promise 'you will be like God' (Genesis 3:5 RSV). In the wilderness, the direct temptations of Satan to Jesus included an appeal to pride, to cast Himself down from the pinnacle of the temple and make a public display of His power. It has been said that pride is the idolatrous worship of ourselves and that is the national religion of hell.

But there is something else that helps us to explain the use of this terrible word 'resisteth', and that is that pride robs God of the glory that is exclusively due to Him. John the Baptist gave us such clear directions here when he said of Jesus, 'He must increase but I must decrease' (John 3:30). Both could not increase together. Watchman Nee, that remarkable man of God, once wrote 'The Christ we manifest is too small because in ourselves we have grown too big. May God forgive us!' God resists the proud, and this is as true for those who are saved as for those who are unsaved. What is more, the principles of resistance are similar.

How then does God resist the proud? He does so in many ways. As Thomas Manton wrote, 'The proud man hath his tactics, and God hath His anti-tactics'! Far from being merely quaint, that verse has a remarkably modern ring about it today in our world of missiles and anti-missiles and anti-missile missiles! Man can go on multiplying his defence against the attacks of his fellow men, but man has no ultimate answer to the tactics and activities of God. How then does God resist man?

Firstly, by refusing to speak. Luke records this very illuminating incident during the trials Jesus faced immediately before His crucifixion – 'And when Herod saw Jesus, he was exceeding glad: for he was desirous to see Him of a long season, because he had heard many things of Him; and he hoped to have seen some miracle done by Him. Then he questioned Him in many words; *but He answered him nothing'* (Luke 23:8–9). Herod was an Edomite, a descendent of Esau, and one of his marked characteristics was pride. But in response to the pride of Herod, Jesus refused to speak. There is a terrible, and much more widely involved example of this in Romans 1, and especially the passage from verse 18 to verse 32. You will discover in that passage that three times God acted in this way towards certain people. We read that 'God also gave them up' (v. 24); that 'God gave them up' (v. 26); and that 'God gave them over' (v. 28). In other words, terrible as it may sound, there came a time when God did nothing to stop them. He refused to speak. Notice too, in that same passage, just who these people were to whom God refused to speak. They were those who went about 'professing themselves to be wise' (v. 22); they 'served the creature more than the Creator' (v. 25); they 'did not like to retain God in their knowledge' (v. 28); and their arrogance is specifically identified by one simple word – they were 'proud' (v. 30). Surely we should tremble at the remotest possibility that even as Christians, we should so plan and conduct our lives that we incur God's terrible silence. God resists the proud, firstly by refusing to speak.

Secondly, by ridiculing their schemes. – This is so clearly brought out by these words from the Psalmist – 'Why do the nations conspire, and the peoples plot in vain? The kings of the earth set themselves, and the rulers take counsel together, against the Lord and His annointed, saying "Let us burst their bonds asunder, and cast their cords from us". He who sits in the heavens laughs; the Lord has them in derision' (Psalm 2:1–4 RSV). This kind of language is known as anthropomorphism (using human terms to describe divine action or attributes). But how telling it is! There is something pathetic about the contrast between men and nations conspiring together and God sitting serenely in the heavens, unmoved except to derisory laughter. To take counsel without the Lord is to take counsel against Him, to think and act as if man can 'go it alone'. The result, sooner or later, is that man discovers that his arm is too short to fight against God. God ridicules their schemes.

Thirdly, by ruining their success. I have always been greatly struck by the story of King Uzziah in 2 Chronicles 26. In the opening verses of the chapter we are told of his great achievements as a king and as an administrator. The story of his great success continues right until the middle of verse 15, when we read, 'And his name spread far abroad; for he was marvellously helped, till he was strong. But when he was strong, his heart was lifted up to his destruction: for he transgressed against the Lord his God, and went into the temple of the Lord to burn incense upon the altar of incense'. He was a king yet he took on himself the function of a priest, strictly reserved for the Levites. Moreover, he did so with the warning of scripture to guard him against this very thing. God had said to Aaron, 'And behold, I have taken your brethren the Levites from among the people of Israel; they are a gift to you, given to the Lord, to do the service of the tent of meeting. And you and your sons shall attend to your priesthood for all that concerns the altar and that is within the veil; and you shall serve. I give your priesthood as a gift, and any one else who comes near shall be put to death' (Numbers 18:6–7 RSV). The result was not only that he was turned out of the sanctuary, but that leprosy struck him and he could not even live in his own palace. His pride was the flame that turned the mighty Uzziah's success to ashes. God resists the proud by ruining their success.

Fourthly, by removing their status. The story of Belshazzar's feast in Daniel 5 is so well known that one hardly needs to set the scene. Here was another king, magnificent in his splendour and almost obscene in his arrogance. Yet, like Uzziah, he also had history to warn him. Daniel reminded him that although his father, Nebuchadnezzar, had been a mighty man, 'when his heart was lifted up, and his mind hardened in pride, he was deposed from his kingly throne, and they took his glory from him' (Daniel 5:20). But even this was not a deterrent to Belshazzar. He went on in his arrogance, but for him too – literally in this case – the writing was on the wall, and in the midst of his revelling he was violently done to death. The Lord has power to give but He also has power to take away, and He does both. None of our posts are so secure that God cannot end them. If we have a position in business, in social life, in the church or anywhere else, we should praise God for it and honour Him in it. These things are written for our learning. If we will not be humbled, then we may have to be humiliated! 'For though the Lord is high, he regards the lowly; but the haughty he knows from afar' (Psalm 138:6 RSV). The first law by which the grace of God is governed is this – the proud in spirit are resisted.

(2) *The poor in spirit are rewarded* – 'but giveth grace unto the humble'. This too is true for the unbeliever and for the believer. It applies both to becoming a Christian and being one, for entrance into the kingdom of God and exaltation in it. Both these applications of the truth are seen in these words of Jesus – 'Verily I say unto you, except ye be converted, and become as little children, ye shall not enter into the kingdom of heaven. Whosoever therefore shall

humble himself as this little child, the same is the greatest in the kingdom of heaven' (Matthew 18:3-4).

The first of those verses applies the truth to the matter of entering the kingdom, of becoming a Christian. To do so, a man must become as a little child, he must humble himself, he must thrust aside all trust in his own efforts or goodness, and throw himself as a spiritual bankrupt upon the mercy of God in Christ. The first of the Beatitudes is 'Blessed are the poor in spirit, for theirs is the kingdom of heaven' (Matthew 5:3) and the particular word translated 'poor' there does not mean having very little, it means having *nothing!* Grace can only be placed into empty hands. A man can only enter into the kingdom of heaven when he comes in the spirit of Augustus Toplady's well-known words

> *Nothing in my hand I bring,*
> *Simply to Thy cross I cling;*
> *Naked, come to Thee for dress;*
> *Helpless, look to Thee for grace;*
> *Foul, I to the fountain fly;*
> *Wash me, Saviour, or I die!*

The second of the verses shows us that the same requirement for blessing remains true when a person has become a Christian, when he is a member of the kingdom of heaven – 'Whosoever therefore shall humble himself . . . is the greatest in the kingdom of heaven'. It was Jesus again who said 'he who is least among you all is the one who is great' (Luke 9:48 RSV). Humility is the key that unlocks the treasures of God's grace. In Christian circles, we so often tend to estimate a man by his gifts – of organisation, oratory, leadership, and so on. But God looks above all for humility, for self-confessed poverty of spirit, and He rewards it not necessarily with outward greatness, but always with inward grace. In the deepest, spiritual sense, the words of the Bible prove to be unshakeably true – 'The reward for humility and fear of the Lord is riches and honour and life' (Proverbs 22:4 RSV).

Chapter 5

VICTORY SECRETS

*'Submit yourselves therefore to God. Resist the devil,
and he will flee from you.'*   (James 4:7)

As a young Christian, this verse used to fascinate me – at
least, that last part of it did! 'Resist the devil, and he will
flee from you', was what I read and the very thought that
that could be my experience when I was a mere beginner in
the Christian life used to stir me to great excitement. Surely
that was what the verse said? After all, it was not given just
to great theologians or mighty Christian warriors who had
been in the battle for many years. This was for *me*, to a
novice, a beginner in the faith – 'the devil will flee from you'.
I could hardly believe my eyes! Of course what I very soon
discovered, from my own experience, and also from a closer
look at the text, was that that phrase came at the end of the
verse and not at the beginning. Other things would need to
come first!

That is the consistent scriptural picture. Paul speaks about
being 'able to withstand in the evil day, and having done
all, to stand' (Ephesians 6:13) – but only after he has said
'Wherefore take unto you the whole armour of God'. Again,
he promises that 'ye shall be able to quench all the fiery
darts of the wicked' (Ephesians 6:16) – but only after
'Above all, taking the shield of faith'. In those two passages,
as here in the Epistle of James, there are certain requirements that must be met before we can experience the
promised result. Let us look at our verse with that pattern
in mind.

1. *THE REQUIREMENTS* – 'Submit yourselves therefore
to God. Resist the devil ...'.

There are two clear requirements here. Let us take them
just as they stand.

(1) *'Submit yourselves therefore to God'*. No sentence
with the word 'submit' in it is likely to be very popular in

this latter part of the 20th Century. We live in what may be an age of unparalleled rebellion. Children rebel against their parents, scholars against their teachers, students against their tutors, workers against their management. All over the world this has led to disturbance, violence, bloodshed and death. It seems to be the very spirit of the age in which we live, a spirit of arrogance, assertion, and self-seeking. Today's slogan is not 'submit yourselves', but 'assert yourselves' – make your own case, stand up for yourself, promote your own ends, and be prepared to destroy anything that stands in your way. During recent trouble at a British University, a student leader said 'we will stop at nothing. Our aim is to destroy the system'.

What a different spirit we find in the pages of the Bible! That great commandment to 'be filled with the Spirit' (Ephesians 5:18) is immediately followed by a series of participles, the last general one of which says 'submitting yourselves one to another in the fear of God' (Ephesians 5:21), or, as The Living Bible puts it, 'Honour Christ by submitting to each other'. Notice very carefully that the mark of a Spirit-filled man is not assertion, but submission. 'Be filled with the Spirit . . . submitting yourselves one to another'. The mark of a Spirit-filled man is not that he struts around boasting of his spiritual superiority, but that he has a spirit of submission, humility and grace.

Of course the perfect example of a Spirit-filled man is the Lord Jesus Christ. Notice what was said about Him when He was rising into His teenage years, and living with His parents at Nazareth. We read that He was 'subject unto them' (Luke 2:51). That is a very significant phrase, because there were two reasons that Jesus could have advanced for not submitting to His parents. First of all, as a Jewish boy he reached his majority on his twelfth birthday, and having reached that age, he could have said 'I will not submit to my parents any more. I am no longer legally bound to them in that way. I can now live my own life, and go my own way'. Secondly, He knew that Joseph was not His father, and He could have refused to submit to him on those grounds. But Jesus, in His home life as in every other part of His earthly life, set up the perfect example, and he was 'subject unto them'.

When we turn to the teaching sections of the Bible, those passages that specifically tell us how we should behave as Christians, we discover again and again that we are commanded to submit ourselves one to another.

In civic matters, for instance, Peter says 'Submit yourselves to every ordinance of man for the Lord's sake . . .' (1 Peter 2 : 13). In simple and general terms, a Christian should be known and recognised as a good citizen. He should submit to the laws and regulations of the country in which he lives, knowing that they are basically there for the promotion of the country's welfare.

In church matters, we are told 'obey them that have the rule over you, and submit yourselves . . .' (Hebrews 13 : 17). In other words, a Christian should be able to discern spiritual leadership in the church, and be willing to submit to it.

In family matters, the Bible says 'Children obey your parents in the Lord: for this is right' (Ephesians 6 : 1). Teaching their children a biblical spirit of submission is one of the most important responsibilities of any parents; obeying it is the most healthy response any child could make.

In business matters, the Bible says 'Servants, obey in all things your masters according to the flesh . . .' (Colossians 3 : 22). What a difference that kind of attitude would make in an age when everybody wants to be the boss, and to take the law into his own hands!

In all these areas, the Bible says that we are to submit ourselves to those who are properly in authority over us, and sums it all up by saying that we should honour Christ by submitting ourselves to each other. Surely that is fitting for those who claim to be followers of the Lord Jesus, for we are told of Him that 'being found in human form He humbled Himself . . .' (Philippians 2 : 8 RSV). To follow His example is also to obey His clear command, 'Take my yoke upon you, and learn of me; for I am meek and lowly in heart: and ye shall find rest unto your souls' (Matthew 11 : 29).

If this principle of submission is so obviously right in our relationships with each other, then how much more should

we be submissive when we turn our faces towards God! –
'Submit yourselves therefore to God'. Let us look briefly at
three biblical reasons to underline this obvious truth.

Firstly, because He is the Lord. Because God is the Lord,
we should submit ourselves to Him. It is as simple as that;
an open and shut case. Listen to Paul's argument – 'But
who are you, a man, to answer back to God? Will what is
moulded say to its moulder "Why have you made me
thus?" ' (Romans 9:20 RSV). Paul is using the illustration
of clay and the potter, and the vessel being made, and he asks
whether it is likely, feasible, sensible or rational that the
vessel when made should rise from the potter's wheel and
complain to the potter about its size, or shape, or intended
use! Why, Paul says, the thing is ludicrous, it is unthinkable.
When the potter takes the clay in his hands he has the right
to do with it whatever he wants. He is the undisputed master
of the situation. In a very much deeper way, because God
is not only the Lord of our human clay, but the Maker of it
in the first place, He has the right to demand our submission
and obedience. Whatever the circumstances of your life, one
general factor remains the same: you are His creature and
He is your Creator. He is the Lord, and therefore He has
the right to decide all the issues of your life, and to demand
your unqualified submission and obedience.

Secondly, because of His law. I do not just mean the law
which forms the text we are studying, 'Submit yourselves
therefore to God', although that is a very clear commandment. I refer rather to the outworking of the law of God
that we find, for instance, in verse 6 – 'Wherefore he saith,
God resisteth the proud'. That, as we saw in our previous
study, is a law. God deliberately sets Himself in array against
the proud man. That is true in the matter of a man who is
not a Christian. He hears the gospel, he is told that in order
to be brought into a saving knowledge of Christ he has to
repent of his sin, he has to recognise that there is nothing
whatever he can do to earn his own salvation, and he has to
receive Christ by faith as a little child. And when he hears
that kind of message he says 'I refuse. I am going to earn
my own salvation. I am going my own way, and trust that
somehow, at the end of the day, God will accept me for

what I have done'. He asserts himself proudly in the face of God and says 'I will save myself'. And when a man takes that attitude, God resists him. Surely that is obvious. God has nothing to say to the proud, arrogant, self-sufficient sinner, But the same law operates in the life of the Christian. He can never lose his salvation, but he can lose a great deal of blessing and fruitfulness by pride in life and service.

Does that explain why we have the word 'therefore' in our verse? – 'Submit yourselves *therefore* to God'. James has been saying that God resists the proud. All history proves it, the Old Testament shows it, your own lives demonstrate it. God resists the proud, *therefore* submit to God. It is sheer commonsense to do so, because of God's law which says that He resists the proud. We should submit ourselves to God because He is the Lord, because of His law, and

Thirdly, because of His love. Here is the other side of the picture. Look at the beginning and the end of verse 6 – 'But He giveth more grace. . . . (He) giveth grace unto the humble'. James is emphasising here the love of God, the mercy of God, the tenderness of God, God's longing to bless His people, to strengthen them, and to guide them. Again using the word 'therefore' as a link, James is saying here that in the light of the love of God and the willingness and the longing of God to help you and to bless you, surely the sensible thing to do is to submit to Him.

So much for the reasons why we should submit to God. But we need to take the matter further, because to say 'submit yourselves therefore to God' is a rather vague and indefinite kind of phrase. We need to ask ourselves the practical question 'In what ways should we do this?' Let us look at three of the answers that can be given.

Firstly, we must submit to His doctrines. It is very interesting to notice people's reactions to the teachings of Jesus. There were occasions when 'the common people heard Him gladly' (Mark 12:37) – but this was not always the case. At one stage we read that many of his disciples murmured at His teaching and said 'This is a hard saying; who can listen to it?' (John 6:60 RSV). A few verses later, after Jesus had taught that nobody could be saved unless he was granted faith by God, we read that 'From that time many of His disciples went back, and walked no more with Him' (John 6:66). That is a most significant phrase! When we talk of disciples we usually think of a handful of people in the New Testament – all of them Christians, but when we do use the term in that rather exclusive way we find ourselves in trouble, because here were disciples who 'walked no more with Him', and that would mean that as Christians they took a course of action which lost them their salvation – something the Bible teaches as impossible. We begin to unravel the problem when we realise that the word 'disciple' very simply meant 'learner', and was a common word in New Testament times. There were disciples of Greek philosophers, Jewish rabbis and many other teachers or professors. They were learners. They were interested in what these people had to teach – but there was not necessarily a personal commitment. If a time came when they could no longer accept the teaching they were being given, they would leave their teacher perhaps to become a disciple of someone else. That is just what happened here. Multitudes flocked to hear what Jesus was teaching, and while He was performing miracles, healing the sick, feeding the hungry, and raising the dead, I have no doubt that there were many of them who were, on the surface at least, 'disciples'. But when Jesus began to teach doctrines that stripped away the pride and the arrogance of man, when He began to show that a man could only be saved when he cast himself wholeheartedly on the grace and mercy of God, many of them drifted away, never to return. They were disciples, they were learners, they were superficial listeners – but they set the limits of what they were prepared to accept and believe. Is the point becoming clear? A disciple must be governed by what he is taught. He must submit to it, and to submit to God includes to submit to His doctrines, to the Word. Jesus said 'If ye continue in my word, *then* are ye my disciples indeed' (John 8:31). Submission to His doctrine was to indicate the reality of discipleship. When we come to the Bible we are to stand under it, even when we cannot understand it! It is not enough for a man to have sincere but vague feelings about God. He must submit to His doctrines, in other words to the teaching of the Bible.

Martin Luther said 'My conscience is captive to the Word of God'; and without that statement and that spirit there would have been no Reformation in Europe. Not only must we submit to His doctrine, but

Secondly, we must submit to His disciplines. This very important issue is much too rarely touched on in these days. The result is too many untaught Christians who tend to think that in some vague way God is responsible for all the pleasure there is in the world, and the devil is responsible for all the pain, that God is responsible for the happy experiences of life, and the devil for the harrowing ones, that God is responsible for life's delights and the devil for life's difficulties. But that is a very long way removed from the teaching of the Bible. In the first place, God is in control of everything that happens in the world. There are no accidents as far as God is concerned. In the second place God often uses disciplines, the hard things of life, pain, sorrow and depravation, to bring about His glory and His people's blessing. That is the plain teaching of scripture – 'Know then in your heart that, as a man disciplines his son, the Lord your God disciplines you' (Deuteronomy 8:5 RSV); 'Behold, happy is the man whom God reproves; therefore despise not the chastening of the Almighty' (Job 5:17 RSV); 'My son, do not regard lightly the discipline of the Lord, nor lose courage when you are punished by Him. For the Lord disciplines him whom He loves, and chastises every son whom He receives' (Hebrews 12:5–6 RSV).

So we should submit to God's disciplines. We should not complain about them, but accept them as coming from His sovereign and all-wise hand. There are two extraordinary examples of this in the Old Testament. The first concerns Eli, who was the priest at Shiloh. His two sons, Hophni and Phinehas, served in the temple there but were guilty of the most terrible sin, sin in which Eli shared because of his failure to exercise restraint over them. The prophet Samuel was given a vision, which he communicated to Eli, and which forecast a terrible visitation from God, during which both Hophni and Phinehas would be killed in one day. When Eli heard the message, his response was this, 'It is the Lord, let Him do what seems good to Him' (1 Samuel 3:18 RSV). We can hardly commend Eli for conniving at his son's blasphemous behaviour – but what a remarkable response to the Lord's disciplining hand upon him!

The other example is the better known one of Job. Job was a man vastly different from Eli. He was 'blameless and upright, one who feared God, and turned away from evil' (Job 1:1). But his integrity was no guarantee that difficulties were not going to come his way, and in one terrible day Job lost all of his flocks, and his ten children were slain. Yet at the end of that day we read that 'Job arose, and rent his mantle, and shaved his head, and fell down upon the ground, and worshipped, and said "Naked came I out of my mother's womb, and naked shall I return thither: the Lord gave, and the Lord hath taken away, blessed be the name of the Lord"' (Job 1:20–21). And the Bible adds, with tremendous significance to the point we are discussing, 'In all this Job sinned not, nor charged God foolishly'. He did not complain against God. He did not charge God with acting unfairly or unjustly towards him. In other words, he submitted to his disciplines.

I remember speaking to some of the Czechoslovakian Pastors who had been imprisoned during the era of Stalin in Moscow and Novotny in Prague, and they told me 'In prison, we learned not to ask "Why?", but just to say "Praise the Lord"'. Can we begin to match the submission of Eli, or Job, or those brave believers in Eastern Europe? Our circumstances may never match theirs – but life does have its disciplines, and we must face up honestly to the question in Josiah Condor's great hymn –

> *The Lord is King! who then shall dare*
> *Resist His will, distrust His care,*
> *Or murmur at His wise decrees.*
> *Or doubt His royal promises?*

Is it not simply and sadly true that in our average daily life we moan and groan at the slightest inconvenience, or difficulty, or restriction? Too often we chafe and complain at even the minor disciplines of life. We can all say 'Praise the Lord!' when the sun is shining and the sky is blue, but when difficulties come into our lives, then we begin to complain, to grow bitter, and even at times to doubt whether God is at work at all. When we do that sort of thing we are not submitting to His disciplines.

Thirdly, we must submit to His demands. This hardly needs saying in view of all that has gone before, but let us just use one illustration to crystallise the truth. When the wine ran out at the marriage at Cana of Galilee, the servants were distraught, but the mother of Jesus knew where the answer lay – 'Do whatever He tells you' (John 2:5 RSV). Every Christian should make that a motto for life! This is the essence of submitting to God in practical terms. It means obeying immediately, wholeheartedly, and without question all of God's revealed will for you. There is a great deal of the will of God for your life that is obviously unknown to you at this moment – it lies in the future – and there is therefore no practical way in which you can submit to it. But there are things that God *has* revealed to you in your life and the crucial question is whether at this moment you are consciously obedient to that which God has revealed to you through His word, by His Spirit, through the fellowship and counsel of other Christians, or in some other way.

To submit to God is the first requirement for victorious Christian living. The second is this –

(2) *'Resist the devil'* The word 'resist' is actually a defensive word, not the same as that used of God in verse 6. The Amplified Bible adds the phrase 'Stand firm against the devil'. Peter uses the same word when he says that the devil is someone we are to 'resist, steadfast in the faith' (1 Peter 5:9). Now there are lessons we can learn from the very nature of the word.

Firstly, the Christian never has to go and pick a fight with the devil. We are told to *resist* the devil, not to go out and attack him. The point seems to be quite clear. If you are a Christian, then the devil is already in the field as 'your adversary' (1 Peter 5:8). He is constantly taking the initiative, fighting you, coming at you. What you have to do is to defend, to resist him. You were born a child of the devil and an enemy of God, and when you become a child of God the devil became your enemy. Mark that carefully! He is your adversary. You are not in a neutral situation, so that it is up to you whether there is going to be a fight or not. The devil is actively engaged against you – your responsibility is to resist. Every Christian is in the Resistance Movement!

Secondly, it is no coincidence that the command to 'resist the devil' comes after the command 'submit to God'. In Peter's more or less parallel passage we are told 'Humble yourselves therefore under the mighty hand of God, that in due time He may exalt you. Cast all your anxieties on him, for he cares about you' (1 Peter 5:6–7 RSV) – and that is immediately followed by 'Be sober, be watchful. Your adversary the devil prowls around like a roaring lion, seeking someone to devour. Resist him . . .' (1 Peter 5:8–9 RSV). Notice the similarity of order. The reason for it is clear: as soon as you submit to God, the devil will intensify his attack. Consecration and conflict go together, and the greater your determination to submit to God, the greater the attack the enemy will make upon you. If you are content to be a slipshod, couldn't-care-less kind of Christian, then the devil is not going to waste much powder on you, but as soon as you determine that you are going to submit to the Word of God, and to the will of God, and commit yourself to the work of God, then the devil is going to be after you, along any of a thousand avenues of attack. The Bible is crystal clear on this – 'all who desire to live a godly life in Christ Jesus will be persecuted' (2 Timothy 3:12 RSV). The godly Christian lives in the arena, not the armchair! That is the plain teaching of the New Testament, all the way through.

Thirdly, this word 'resist' is not a passive word, but an active one. It is defensive but not docile. It is not a question of 'Let go and let God'. To be submissive is not to be spineless. The Emphasised New Testament, by J. B. Rotherham, brings this out well by translating 'Range yourselves therefore under God'. This is an active, positive word. It is defensive, but dynamic! *'Resist* the devil'!

We are to resist his arguments, for they are always dishonest. Jesus said of the devil 'he is a liar and the father of lies' (John 8:44 RSV). In his first recorded words, in Genesis 3, he disputed the word of God. *We are to resist his attractions,* for they are deceptive. Paul tells the Corinthians that at times 'Satan disguises himself as an angel of light' (2

Corinthians 11:14 RSV). This is true both in matters of belief and behaviour. There is something satanically attractive about false teaching, about grossly unbiblical interpretation. So in the realm of morals and ethics, he offers liberty from all the 'restrictions' of old conventions, ideas and standards; he offers freedom, but brings fetters! *We are to resist his attacks*, for they are always dangerous. Even at his most subtle and gentle, he remains a roaring lion – vicious, cruel, heartless, and callous beyond our imagination. All his attacks, even the smallest, are designed to harm, hurt, and humiliate us. We are to resist him all along the line. But how are we to resist him? As with the matter of submitting ourselves to God, it will be helpful if we look, however briefly, at the answer to that question.

(a) *By not being ignorant of his devices.* The Apostle Paul was able to say 'We are not ignorant of his devices' (2 Corinthians 2:11), and our minds need to be stored with the recorded biblical history of the tactics, devices, policies and arguments which Satan has used against the children of God down the years.

(b) *By not giving him place.* Paul says plainly 'Neither give place to the devil' (Ephesians 4:27) or, as The Amplified Bible puts it, 'Leave no such room or foothold for the devil – give no opportunity to him'. It is important to our understanding of what that means to notice that in the previous verse Paul had commanded the Ephesians 'Be angry but do not sin; do not let the sun go down on your anger' (Ephesians 4:26 RSV). To nurse a grievance is to leave the door open for other sins. There is a lesson here we need to learn! Sins seldom go alone; one leads to another. Of course there is another sense in which we are not to give the devil place or opportunity, and that is by carefully avoiding things, places, or situations that bring obvious exposure to our own personal weaknesses. The devil knows your Achilles heel. Be sure to keep your shoes on!

(c) *By putting on the whole armour of God.* The teaching on this is of course found in Ephesians 6, to which we have already referred several times. To go into it in detail would transfer our study from James to Paul, so let me just quote the whole of the relevant passage, from a modern version that

might help to bring its vital impact home in a fresh way –
'Put on all of God's armour so that you will be able to
stand safe against the strategies and tricks of Satan. For we
are not fighting against people made of flesh and blood, but
against persons without bodies – the evil rulers of the unseen
world, those mighty satanic beings and great evil princes of
darkness who rule this world; and against huge numbers of
wicked spirits in the spirit world. *So use every piece of God's
armour to resist the enemy whenever he attacks,* and when
it is all over, you will still be standing up. But to do this,
you will need the strong belt of truth and the breastplate of
God's approval. Wear shoes that are able to speed you on
as you preach the Good News of peace with God. In every
battle you will need faith as your shield to stop the fiery
arrows aimed at you by Satan. And you will need the helmet
of salvation and the sword of the Spirit – which is the Word
of God' (Ephesians 6 : 11–17 The Living Bible).

Those, then, are the two requirements. We are to submit
ourselves to God, and we are to resist the devil. If we do, we
can claim the second part of the verse –

2. *THE RESULT* – 'he will flee from you'.

We have approached this point very slowly, but there the
promise stands! – 'he *will* flee from you'. In closing our
study, let me draw your attention to three important in-
ferences we can draw from this.

(1) *The devil is vulnerable.* The New English Bible translates this phrase 'he will turn and run'! In his book 'The
Invisible War', Donald Grey Barnhouse has a section on
'The ignorance of Satan' in which he argues that although
the devil is 'the wisest creature ever to come from the Word
of God' and has 'retained the wisdom of Lucifer, in a perverted sense, he most certainly is not omniscient'. Barnhouse goes on to say that there are at least two things Satan
does not know – 'he does not know what goes on within the
mind and heart of man, and he does not know the future'.
Whether or not one agrees with the examples Barnhouse
gives, he is surely right to speak of 'The ignorance of Satan'.
There are things Satan does not know, and there are things
he cannot do. That makes him vulnerable! He is strong, but

not supreme, he is potent but he is not omnipotent. He can be beaten back, forced to give ground. He is vulnerable!

(2) *We must be vigilant.* The devil can be defeated, but he is never defeated once and for all in the course of a man's lifetime. In the narrative of the wilderness temptation endured by Jesus, we are told 'And when the devil had ended all the temptation, he departed from him for a season' (Luke 4:13), or as The Amplified Bible most helpfully puts it, 'he left Him temporarily, that is, stood off from Him until another more opportune and favourable time'. Mark that carefully! He did not leave Jesus once and for all. When Jesus had inflicted those tremendous blows upon him, Satan turned and ran. He left Him – but not for ever; only until a more convenient time came to attack again. And although there is going to come a time for every Christian when 'the God of peace shall bruise Satan under your feet' (Romans 16:20); although it shall be said of us as it is said of multitudes in heaven, 'they overcame him by the blood of the Lamb, and by the word of their testimony' (Revelation 12:11), the fact of the matter is that here on earth he is going to win as many battles and inflict as many wounds and cause as much damage as he possibly can. So we must be vigilant! We must be constantly on our guard.

William Grimshaw of Howarth said 'I expect to lay down my life and my sword together'. Someone else put it like this, 'In the fight, we should have an eye to victory, and in the victory to the fight again'. We must be vigilant!

(3) *We can be victorious.* The text says so! – 'the devil *will* flee from you'. Our posture is to be defensive but not defeatist. Many of today's protest marches sing variations on a song with the refrain 'We shall overcome some day'. Sometimes, depending on the cause, that hope sounds so vague, so improbable, and so far distant. The Christian, on the other hand, is able to sing a much greater song, one that says 'I *can* overcome *today*'! We can be 'more than conquerors through Him Who loved us' (Romans 8:37 RSV). We *can* be victorious, we can know the joy of temptation overcome, of new heights gained, of progress made, of victories achieved. And when we do, let us remember to give the glory to God. For God to defeat Satan demonstrates His

greatness, but for God to enable us to defeat him demonstrates His grace!

Charles Wesley gives us just the words with which to close this study –

> *Jesu's tremendous Name*
> *Puts all our foes to flight:*
> *Jesus the meek, the angry Lamb,*
> *A Lion is in fight.*
> *By all hell's host withstood,*
> *We all hell's host o'erthrow;*
> *And conquering them, through Jesu's blood,*
> *We still to conquer go!*

Chapter 6

THE CHRISTIAN'S WALK WITH GOD

*'Draw nigh to God, and he will draw nigh to you.
Cleanse your hands, ye sinners; and purify your hearts,
ye double minded. Be afflicted, and mourn, and weep:
let your laughter be turned to mourning, and your joy
to heaviness.'*
(James 4 : 8–9)

If there is a particular thrill to the Christian in reading the
end of verse 7, which we examined in the previous chapter,
then there is an equal thrill about the beginning of verse 8,
to which we now turn. There is a wonderful 'lift' in it all –
'Resist the devil and he will flee from you. Draw nigh to
God and He will draw nigh to you'. There are two views the
Christian ought to covet more than any other; one is Satan's
back and the other is God's face – and these verses promise
us that we can have both of those views!

There are many people in the Bible who walked with the
Lord, and there are two men of whom those very words are
used. We read that 'Enoch walked with God' (Genesis 5 : 24)
and a little later that 'Noah walked with God' (Genesis 6 : 9).
What a lovely phrase to describe the Christian life! It
reminds us immediately that the Christian life is not a matter
of slavishly following rules or rituals, but one of personal
experience and relationship. It is a walk with God. Of
course, as we saw in our last study, there is a need to submit
to God's doctrines, His disciplines and His demands, but
even in doing so, we must not lose sight of the fact that the
Christian life is essentially a living relationship with God
day by day. These two verses tell us four things that should
characterise the Christian's walk with God; three of them
stated in the nature of commandments and one in the nature
of a promise. Let us look at the commandments first,
although this will mean a slight alteration to the order in
which we deal with the phrases forming these verses.

1. *COMMUNION* – 'Draw nigh to God'. The Amplified

Bible translates this 'Come close to God', and as these words
are written to Christians, we might just take a moment to
clear away two possible areas of difficulty arising from the
phrase.

Firstly, do not be puzzled about it. What I mean is this:
somebody might ask 'How can I, as a Christian, be told to
draw nigh to God? I have already done that. That was how
I became a Christian. I drew near to God by putting my
trust in Christ'. Does that seem a little bit puzzling? If it
does, the answer to it is that the Bible does not use just one
illustration of the Christian's relationship with God. The
Bible is prolific in the pictures that it paints, in the descriptions that it gives, in the analogies that it draws to describe
the Christian's position. Some of them, if looked at just on
the surface, would seem to make nonsense of each other.
Let me give you the clearest example of all. The Apostle
Paul tells us that a Christian is 'in Christ' (2 Corinthians
5:17), but elsewhere he speaks of 'Christ in you, the hope
of glory' (Colossians 1:27). On the surface, that would seem
to be a glaring contradiction – but in fact both statements
are accurate and each holds a wealth of spiritual truth for
the believer. To illustrate in another way, the Bible in one
place says that the church is 'the bride, the Lamb's wife'
(Revelation 21:9). In another place it speaks of 'the church,
which is His body' (Ephesians 1:22–23). Elsewhere, we discover that Christians are described as 'brethren of the Lord'
(1 Corinthians 5:9). Now in human terms, of course, those
things are mutually exclusive. You cannot at one and the
same time be a person's bride, body and brother! But the
Bible does not limit its illustrations to one. It gives many –
each of which opens up one particular facet of truth. So
when, as a Christian, you read 'Draw nigh to God', do not
be puzzled!

Secondly, do not be presumptuous about it. The point to
emphasise here is that while every Christian is eternally
secure, there is a constant, daily need to 'draw nigh to God'.
It is not something that happens automatically. We are not
computerised into maturity. No amount of knowledge or
service can guarantee it. Our communion must be cultivated.
Take the illustration of marriage again. People get married

in a moment of time, but if that marriage is going to succeed the marriage bond needs to be cultivated. It needs to be worked at, or the relationship will cool. This is why the Psalmist says 'It is good for me to draw near to God' (Psalm 73:28), and why the Bible exhorts 'Let us draw near with a true heart in full assurance of faith' (Hebrews 10:22). The daily prayer of every Christian should be in the spirit of Mrs C. H. Morris's hymn –

> *Nearer, still nearer, close to Thy heart,*
> *Draw me, my Saviour, so precious Thou art;*
> *Fold me, O fold me close to Thy breast,*
> *Shelter me safe in that haven of rest.*

Here, in this opening phrase of verse 8, is a definite, specific and continual command for us to draw near to God. We are not just to assume that because we belong to an evangelical church, because we hear sound ministry of the Word, because we go through the ritual of a quiet time every day, because we read the Bible, that we are automatically making progress in the Christian life. Progress in the Christian life is never automatic. Progress is a matter of cultivated communion.

2. *CLEANSING* – 'Cleanse your hands, ye sinners; and purify your hearts, ye double minded' (v. 8). These words could obviously be addressed to people who are unconverted, but let us remember that originally they were written to Christians. What is equally clear, however, is that at this point he especially had in mind Christians who were out of conscious, happy, daily touch with the Lord. In a word, they were backsliders. This gave James a particular reason for calling them 'sinners'. Although saved by grace, they were sinners by disgrace! – out of conscious, living touch with the Lord.

James seems to have two groups in mind here, or perhaps he has two ways of describing one group of people. In any event, both are closely linked. Notice the two faults he discovers here:

(1) *Dirty hands* – 'Cleanse your hands'. The first thing to say is that this is not a question of hygiene. We will get quickly to the truth if we remember that in the Bible the

hands are symbolic of the outward actions. In the Old
Testament, the priests' ritual in preparation for drawing
near to the Ark of God always included the washing of
hands. Now beyond any shadow of doubt his hands would
already have been clean. Yet he would still go through an
elaborate and deliberate ritual of washing his hands in the
sight of the people. Why? Because it was a *visual aid*. It
demonstrated the holiness of God. It showed that man could
not come into God's presence with dirty hands – that is to
say, with unconfessed sin. Later on the meaning developed to
take in the actual removal of moral defilement. David cried
'I wash my hands in innocence' (Psalm 26:6 RSV); while
after the trial of Jesus, Pilate 'took water, and washed his
hands before the multitude, saying, "I am innocent of the
blood of this just person, see ye to it" ' (Matthew 27:24).

Now when we think of walking with the Lord in terms of
the word 'communion', we probably tend to think first of
the Lord's supper and prayer, and it is interesting to see how
hands fit in with those two things, both by illustration and
by biblical statement. Speaking about our coming to the
Lord's table Paul warns 'Let a man examine himself' (1
Corinthians 11:28). Will a man come to this sacred reminder
of the death of the Lord with dirty hands, with unconfessed
sin? Surely not! Let a man be sure that his sin is confessed
and put away before he dares come to this place where communion with the Lord is visually demonstrated.

Then the matter of prayer. Paul says 'I will therefore that
men pray every where, lifting up holy hands without wrath
and doubting' (1 Timothy 2:8). Now there are Christians
who instead of bowing their heads and perhaps folding their
hands when they pray, lift or wave their hands above their
heads, presumably with this verse as a mandate. While I
could not personally find specific warrant for that in these
words of Paul, I am sure that to lift the hands in prayer is
perfectly harmless – some might even find it helpful – but
what is manifestly clear is that the all important word in this
verse is the word 'holy'. Better to pray with your hands
hanging down but with your sins confessed and forgiven
than to wave them around in some kind of ecstatic
demonstration of pseudo-spirituality and to have uncon-

fessed sin nullifying it all. The real point is not that you
lift up your hands but that your hands are holy, in other
wards that your sin is confessed. Dirty hands speak of unconfessed sin, and there can be no close walk with God
unless your sin is confessed and forsaken. As we saw in an
earlier study, the Bible makes that quite clear – 'If I regard
iniquity in my heart, the Lord will not hear me' (Psalm
66:18). Incidentally, the Bible's usual word for 'confess'
comes from two words meaning 'same' and 'speak'. To
confess sin to God is to speak about it in the same way that
He does, to call it by the same name. Many of us who are
evangelicals, and who revel in our great insistence upon
justification by faith and by faith alone, can so easily slide
into that area of Christian living where we forget that God
is concerned about particulars. It is so easy to pray 'O Lord
forgive our sins!' and to leave it at that. And God *does*
forgive sin, in a wonderful and immediate way. God does not
answer us because of our multiplication of words. But let us
not for that reason fall into the error of failing to be specific
when it comes to the confession of our failures and sins.. Let
us not be content with wrapping up our confession in
generalities. We sin in deliberate ways, we sin in paritcular
ways, we sin in individual ways. There are words we say,
things we do, thoughts that pass through our minds that are
sinful. Then as the Holy Spirit reveals them to us as such,
let us know something of the deep sorrow of confessing those
individual sins before God and the deep joy of knowing His
cleansing away of each one of them individually! James's
first complaint, then, is about dirty hands. But he has
another –

(2) *Divided hearts* – 'and purify your hearts, ye double
minded'. This speaks not so much of outward actions but of
inward affections. The Amplified Bible translates the phrase
'realise that you have been disloyal, wavering individuals
with divided interests, and purify your hearts of your
spiritual adultery'. That takes us back to James 4:4, where
he calls these people 'adulterers and adulteresses', unfaithful
creatures who deserted their true spiritual Husband. The
phrase 'double minded' is an unusual one. It is only used
by James, and then only here and in chapter 1 verse 8. The

order of the phrases in the verse we are studying – hands
first and then heart – is the same as where the prophet Isaiah
says 'Let the wicked forsake his way, and the unrighteous
man his thoughts: and let him return unto the Lord' (Isaiah
55:7). The 'hands' and 'ways' come first (perhaps they are
mentioned first because they are noticed first), but ultimately
we get back to the heart. This is precisely why we are warned
'Keep thy heart with all diligence; for out of it are the issues
of life' (Proverbs 4:23). In counselling people in spiritual
need, I find so often that the trouble seems to lie not so much
in a specific action, something that people can identify, but
rather in a general unspiritual attitude, what Guy King
called 'worldliness, that unworthy division of the affections'.

In all of this, there are two things of which we can be
certain. The first is that God knows the truth about us. He
says 'I the Lord search the heart' (Jeremiah 17:10). The
second is that He demands our total allegiance – 'You shall
worship the Lord your God, and Him only shall you serve'
(Matthew 4:8 RSV). And that, incidentally, was the scripture quoted by Jesus when Satan was trying to divide His
heart! But let me add a necessary word of caution here. In
urging people to be committed to the Lord with an un-
divided heart, some preachers thunder out this kind of
challenge – 'Are you 100% for God' or 'Are you 100% for
Jesus Christ'? Whenever I hear a preacher say that sort of
thing, I must say that I cringe, not because I know the sad
answer I must give, but because the man ought never to be
preaching like that. It is an unfair question, because the
Christian life is not a matter of percentages. It is a living,
growing, developing relationship, and because one of the
partners is fallible and human and subject to temptation,
then it is an imperfect relationship, and it will remain so as
long as we are here in the flesh upon earth. Grasp that! –
because it is tremendously important. To fail to do so is to
find yourself in an area of 'perfectionism' that will bring
nothing but frustration in the end. There can be a kind of
spiritual temperature-taking that is morbid, introspective
and counter-productive.

Nevertheless, we need to be sure that we do not have
divided hearts. 'Blessed are the pure in heart for they shall

see God' (Matthew 5:8). Søren Kierkegaard, the 19th Century Danish theologian, once said, 'Purity of heart is to will one thing', and that points us surely in the right direction. Frances Ridley Havergal put her own aspirations in these lovely words –

> Jesus, Master, whose I am,
> Purchased Thine alone to be;
> By Thy blood, O spotless Lamb,
> Shed so willingly for me;
> Let my heart be all Thine own,
> Let me live to Thee alone.

Not only should the Christian's walk with God be characterised by communion and cleansing, but also by –

3. *CONCERN* – 'Be afflicted, and mourn, and weep: let your laughter be turned to mourning, and your joy to heaviness' (v. 9).

Whatever else we may discover to be true about this phrase, it is certainly a long way removed from the spirit of the age in which we live. 'Eat, drink and be merry for tomorrow we die' is for many the whole philosophy of life. We live in an age in which the pursuit of pleasure has become a social obsession. For an increasing number of people, the selfish pursuit of enjoyment is taking up more and more time, energy, money and concern. But the phrase is also a long way removed from a widespread emphasis in some Christian circles today where the all-important goals are joy, peace and happiness, where it is a sin not to be singing all the time, where a man's standard is measured by his smile and his godliness by his grin, and it is almost the unforgivable sin not to be bubbling over in the prescribed manner! This sort of thing can be so superficial and unreal. While the Christian life is a wonderfully happy life, it is not funny. It is not a game, a playful performance. It has its moments, and sometimes its long periods of solemn, searching discipline.

On the other hand, this verse is certainly not a call to a morbid kind of misery, nor a blanket prohibition on fun, relaxation, laughter or enjoyment. The Bible nowhere takes that line. Speaking of God delivering His people from captivity, the Psalmist says 'Then was our mouth filled with laughter, and our tongue with singing' (Psalm 126:2). Bildad promised Job that God would 'fill your mouth with laughter, and your lips with shouting' (Job 8:21 RSV). The Christian who can never smile, never laugh, never have a happy sense of enjoyment, is a Christian who is missing a dimension God intends him to have. Then what is the meaning of these words?

We could spend a great deal of time delving into the precise meaning of the words used here – 'afflicted', 'mourn', 'joy', 'heaviness' and so on, but I want to assume that the verse is saying just one basic and general thing, and that is, especially as we seek to draw near to God, our attitude should be marked by seriousness that we can rightly call concern. Here are three reasons why I say that. We should be concerned

(1) *Because of unrepented sin.* Remember that this is directed to Christians who are out of touch with God, people who are discovering through the probing of the Holy Spirit that they have got dirty hands and divided hearts. The message then becomes clear: when the Holy Spirit exercises that kind of ministry in a man's life, surely there is something wrong if he has no tears to shed. Beware of mechanical prayers – and especially mechanical confession of sin! The following words are written in the General Confession included in the Service of Holy Communion in the Book of Common Prayer, and are therefore said (with no exceptions sufficient to disprove the rule) by every person in the worldwide Anglican Communion, whenever he approaches the moment of receiving the bread and wine – 'Almighty God, Father of our Lord Jesus Christ, Maker of all things, Judge of all men; we acknowledge and bewail our manifold sins and wickedness, which we, from time to time, have most grievously committed, by thought, word and deed against Thy Divine Majesty, provoking most justly Thy wrath and indignation against us. We do earnestly repent, and are heartily sorry for these our misdoings; the remembrance of them is grievous unto us, the burden of them is intolerable . . .'. Those are solemn, searching words – yet I can remember, in my younger, unconverted days, rattling

them off with a smile on my face, with no effort whatever to grasp their meaning, no broken-hearted sense that the words were all too sadly true.

What a contrast we get in the Bible! Job says 'I abhor myself, and repent in dust and ashes' (Job 42:6); Paul cries out 'O wretched man that I am!' (Romans 7:24); — and incidentally the word 'wretched' comes from the same root as the word 'afflicted' here in James — while Peter, in his moment of bitter discovery, 'remembered . . . went out, and wept bitterly' (Matthew 26:75). What James is contending for here is the need for a deep sense of sorrow at our own personal sin when the Holy Spirit reveals it to us. When did you last shed a tear over your own sin, your own failure, your own lukewarmness of heart, your own divided affections? We should have a concern because of unrepented sin, but also

(2) *Because of unrecognised sovereignty.* Frederick P. Wood, one of the founders of the Young Life Campaign, was walking in a town one day with his brother Arthur, when they were engulfed by a crowd of young people coming in the opposite direction. When they finally came through the crowd, Arthur noticed that there were tears in his brother's eyes. 'Why are you crying?' he asked. Frederick hung his head and said slowly 'They don't know my Saviour'. That great saint was not judging them harshly, but there was something about their behaviour, their language, their attitude that convinced that sensitive man of God that they were unbelievers, that they were lost. When did you last weep over anyone who did not know your Saviour? When was there last a single tear in your eye over one person dead in trespasses and sins? When did you last weep with concern over someone within your own home, someone living under your own roof, someone in your family, someone with whom you work, someone with whom you mix socially, and who is away from God, and who but for a miracle of divine grace will spend eternity in hell? You may say that you care, you may pass on literature, you may witness to them, you do all the outward things — but what about the inward things? What about the heart breaking with concern? Can we honestly say that we are walking with God when we have

no concern for people who are lost, and who do not recognise their rightful Sovereign? David was able to say 'My eyes shed streams of tears because men do not keep Thy law' (Psalm 119:136). Of course, even in that condition, the world has its laughter. But can we share in it? Have you noticed the areas from which the humour of the mass media is by and large drawn today? – they are drunkenness, immorality, crime in general and blasphemy. Those are things the world laughs at more than anything else. Can a Christian happily join in? One thing is certain. The Christian who gets his humour from the world does not give honour to the Lord.

Not only is the Lord's sovereignty not recognised in the world, it is also unrecognised to a large extent in the church. The result is that we have the organisational, structured church riddled with heresy, crippled with compromise, ripped and torn by schism. Paul was able to tell the church leaders of his day 'Therefore watch, and remember, that by the space of three years I ceased not to warn everyone night and day with tears' (Acts 20:31). Paul was concerned about the church of his day to the point of weeping. Have we any tears for the church? Most Christians have a voice for the Church, – but too often it is a voice of criticism, of disagreement, of argument, of bitterness, or of division; either that or it is a voice of careless, empty, superficial, comment and gossip. Have we no tears for the church? Are we not concerned about it? – Concerned that it is such a ridiculed, despised, divided minority with so little recognition of its Lord? Let me add one further concern the Christian should have. It is not directly stated in the text but I am sure that the practical, down to earth James would approve of us drawing it into the general need for seriousness and concern, and that is

(3) *Because of unrelieved suffering.* On the day I originally prepared this study, news came over the radio of a plane crash in Spain when over 100 British holidaymakers perished on a lonely mountain. It was a dramatic reminder to me that we live in a world of pain and sorrow, tragedy, agony and suffering, disease, sickness and disaster – in other words a world of unrelieved suffering. But do we *care?* Paul said

'Rejoice with those who rejoice, weep with those who weep' (Romans 12:14 RSV). Are we concerned about the suffering, pain and injustice that is going on around us in the world? Have we no tears for a world of unrelieved suffering? Surely this should be part of the Christian's concern.

One last word climaxes our study of these two verses –
4. *CONFIDENCE.* The Christian's walk with God can be one of confidence – 'And He *will* draw nigh to you'. Seeking to encourage the people of Israel, Moses tells them 'For what great nation is there that has a god so near to it as the Lord our God is to us, whenever we call upon him?' (Deuteronomy 4:7 RSV). Here is the leader of God's people reminding them that while they were such a tiny, insignificant nation in the world's eyes *God was near them when they called upon Him.* That same truth runs like a vein of gold throughout the whole of the Bible. 'The Lord is with you while you are with Him. If you seek Him, He will be found by you' (2 Chronicles 15:2 RSV); 'Return to me, and I will return to you, says the Lord of hosts' (Malachi 3:7 RSV); 'If we say that we have no sin, we deceive ourselves, and the truth is not in us. If we confess our sins, He is faithful and just to forgive us our sins, and to cleanse us from all unrighteousness' (1 John 1:8–9). What wonderful truths these are! It has been pointed out that (although we can never escape their impact) the verbs James uses here are not in the present continuous tense. What that teaches me is this: that we are not to go on confessing the same sins, dragging them up before God again and again. A friend of mine used to say that some Christians have got a spiritual Home Secretary living within them. His point was that in Britain, the Home Secretary is the only man in the country with the right to authorise an exhumation, and that some Christians take a sin to the Lord, confess it, bury it – and then when it starts nagging and worrying them again they order an exhumation, they get the wretched thing up again and confess it again. Then after it has lain buried for a while they start worrying about it yet again, and again they drag it up and go through the same, sad process. Although we must always have a spirit of godly sorrow, we must not fall into the devil's trap and believe his

deadly lie that we can never have a sense of forgiveness and
cleansing and of God drawing near to us with the assurance
of His presence and power. We can – that is the radiant
message shining through the solemn words of these verses.
If we draw nigh to God in the way James says, we can know
His cleansing and forgiveness. We can know that He has
drawn near to us.

One of Basilea Schlink's books has the arresting title
'Repentance – The joy-filled life', and in choosing those
words she has captured so well the Lord's meaning when He
said 'Blessed are those who mourn, for they shall be com-
forted' (Matthew 5:4 RSV). Are you seeking to pursue a
close walk with God? Then come to Him consciously deter-
mined to deepen your communion with Him; come seeking
His cleansing of every area of life that has displeased Him;
come in an attitude of concern about your own short-
comings, about the lost souls who surround you, and all the
agony and suffering of the world in which you live; – and if
you do, you can also come in a spirit of confidence, knowing
that if you draw near to God He will draw near to you and
give you the assurance of His presence.

Chapter 7

HUMILITY

'Humble yourselves in the sight of the Lord, and He shall lift you up.' (James 4:10)

One of the greatest theologians and apologists for the Christian faith outside the pages of the New Testament was undoubtedly Aurelius Augustinius, better known as St Augustine. Converted in the year 387, and later Bishop of Hippo in North Africa, many of his sayings have become classics of Christian expression down the years. One of them is this – 'For those who would learn God's ways, humility is the first thing, humility is the second, and humility is the third'. At first sight, that may seem a somewhat exaggerated statement, yet the more you think it over, the more it is seen to lie at the heart of Christian discipleship.

Our previous study, entitled 'The Christian's Walk with God', covered verses 8–9, but we could so easily allow that title to take in verse 10 with its simple, direct commandment, 'Humble yourselves in the sight of the Lord and He shall lift you up'. To do so would fit exactly into the kind of picture we have again and again in the pages of scripture, and classically in the verse that says 'He has showed you, O man, what is good; and what does the Lord require of you, but to do justice, and to love kindness, and to talk humbly with your God'. (Micah 6:8 RSV). Any element of the Christian's walk with God must include humility; or, to put it in different words, the only way in which a Christian can walk closely with the Lord is to walk humbly with Him. There is no other way. That truth is underlined throughout the Bible. As Dennis Tongue puts it in The New Bible Dictionary, 'The emphasis placed on pride, and its converse humility, is a distinctive feature of biblical religion unparalleled in other religions or ethical systems'. That alone is sufficient to establish its importance, and gives us ample warrant for devoting a whole chapter to this brief verse of just fourteen words.

The verse has two parts, a commandment and a promise. Taking them in that order, notice

1. HOW THE PRINCIPLE IS STRESSED – 'Humble yourselves in the sight of the Lord'.

This is not the first mention in the Epistle of James of the merit of humility or of the menace of pride. Although the words 'proud' and 'humble' are not used until chapter 4 verse 6, both are inferred many times. The point to notice here is how the principle of humility is stressed. This is seen in two ways

(1) *A straightforward manner* – 'Humble yourselves'. James gets straight to the point. There is no beating about the bush, no exceptions are made, no excuses tolerated, no alternatives accepted. 'Humble yourselves', he says. Get down from your pedestal! Cross out the capital 'I'! I wonder whether there are two words in all the New Testament Epistles that are more necessary for the Christian today than these two words 'humble yourselves'. If we were to remove all the texts which festoon our houses and replace them by the two words 'Humble yourselves', so that when we sat down to a meal, when we went into the lounge to talk to other people, when we went into the study to work, we were faced with those same two words, what an impact they might have! Certainly, if they were obeyed they would revolutionise our homes, our churches, our Christian service, indeed the whole of our lives.

Many years ago there was a famous correspondence in 'The Times' under the subject 'What is wrong with the world today?' The best letter of all was also the shortest. It read like this – 'Dear Sir, I am, Yours faithfully, G. K. Chesterton'. That devastating declaration showed a profound insight into man's universal malaise, and I believe that it can teach us a deeply challenging lesson. I am convinced that all over the Christian church there are problems, difficulties and frustrations that would begin to dissolve immediately if only Christians would be honest enough to answer the question – 'What's wrong?' with the words 'I am'!

It is interesting to notice that this verse follows immediately after a verse which speaks of the need for a continuous attitude of repentance and faith on the part of the
Christian. It helps to remind us that even repentance and
faith are not things of which we can be proud. Repentance,
for instance, is a gift. Peter told the authorities at Jerusalem
that God had raised Christ from the dead and exalted Him
'to be a Prince and a Saviour for to *give* repentance to Israel,
and forgiveness of sins' (Acts 5:31). Faith is also a gift.
Jesus said quite plainly 'No man can come unto Me, except
it were *given* unto him of my Father' (John 6:65) We should
be eternally grateful that we are Christians, but never proud!
We can actually take that even further. As Christians, we
are not to be proud of whatever standard that we may have
reached in the quality of our lives. While it should be true
that we are growing in grace and in knowledge, while we
should be grasping more and more of the scriptures, while
our lives should be counting more and more for God and
for good, we must never arrive at the situation where we
are proud of our progress. There is a very fine balance here
that can only be maintained by the work of the Holy Spirit
in our lives – a balance seen so perfectly in Paul's word to
the Corinthians, 'By the grace of God I am what I am' (1
Corinthians 15:10), and in the commandment given by Jesus
in the Sermon on the Mount when He said, 'Let your light
so shine before men, that they may see your good works,
and glorify your Father which is in heaven' (Matthew 5:16).
We must be godly, but He must be glorified! I have said that
James deals with his subject in a straightforward manner,
and so he does. This becomes even clearer when we recognise that the precise grammar would allow us to render
the phrase 'allow yourselves to be humble'. We cannot even
boast of our humility! It is the gift of God, the work of the
Holy Spirit, part of His refining and purifying ministry in
the hearts and lives of believers.

Perhaps there is one area in particular in which James's
words are needed more than any other, and that is in the
realm of Christian service. We have so many offices, ranks
and positions. There are so many committees, councils
within our church organisation – and the human heart being

what it is, we can get so taken up with the position we hold
that we almost obliterate the Christ we are professing to
serve. The Apostle John said of Diotrephes that he 'likes to
put himself first' (3 John 9). That was his main concern. It
was not that he was not gifted, or that he was not busy in
the Lord's service, but he loved what he was doing because
it gave him preeminence, it put him in the forefront of things.
Is there a word to your own heart there? What a contrast
we discover in the life of George Whitefield. Dr Martyn
Lloyd-Jones has called him 'the greatest preacher that England has ever produced', yet Charles Wesley could write this
of him in 1771 –

> *Though long by following multitudes admired,*
> *No party for himself he e'er desired;*
> *His one desire, to make the Saviour known,*
> *To magnify the Name of Christ alone.*
> *If others strove who should the greatest be,*
> *No lover of pre-eminence was he.*

To switch the picture completely, we sometimes speak of
the Christian life as being a fight, a battle, a warfare, and of
those who are serving the Lord in some specific way as being
in the front line of battle. Now in the front line, it is always
safest to keep low! There is always a great danger in standing up and exhibiting yourself when you are in the front line
of battle! Here, then, is the lesson. The secret of true greatness is littleness. The secret of spiritual wealth is poverty of
spirit. One of the last messages of Fred Burgin, Director of
the Muller Homes, included this wise counsel – 'Tell my
younger brethren that they can be too big for God to use, but
they cannot be too small'.

So there is a straightforward manner in which this principle is stressed. 'Humble yourselves'! Let us not try to
evade the sharp edge of those two words with all sorts of
excuses and rationalisation. Every single one of us, without
exception, needs to have these words brought right home to
our hearts. Not only does James speak in a straightforward
manner, he also gives

(2) *A supreme motive.* – 'in the sight of the Lord'. Notice
that he does not say, *'when* you are in the sight of the Lord'

or '*as if* you were in the sight of the Lord'. He simply says '*in* the sight of the Lord' – because we *are!* Have you ever noticed that in the first and last books in the Bible we read of men's futile attempts to escape God's presence? We read of Adam and Eve that, after their fall into sin, 'they heard the voice of the Lord God walking in the garden in the cool of the day: and Adam and his wife hid themselves from the presence of the Lord God among the trees of the garden' (Genesis 3:8). But does that mean that they placed themselves where God could not see them, or know what they had done? Of course not! Then towards the end of the Bible we read of multitudes who, facing judgment, 'hid themselves in the dens and in the rocks of the mountains; and said to the mountains and rocks, "Fall on us, and hide us from the face of Him that sitteth on the throne, and from the wrath of the Lamb"' (Revelation 6:15–16). But can that ever happen? Can mountains and rocks hide anyone from the all-seeing eye of the Judge of all the earth? Of course not! To those two examples, we could add a story from the very heart of the Bible, the story of Jonah, baulking at God's command from him to preach at Ninevah. Terrified of the responsibility being laid upon him, he 'rose up to flee unto Tarshish from the presence of the Lord' (Jonah 1:3). But did he succeed? Did he manage to reach a place so distant that he was inaccessible to God? Of course not! Jonah discovered the inescapable truth that 'all things are naked and opened unto the eyes of Him with whom we have to do' (Hebrews 4:13). No man can escape from the sight and knowledge and presence of God. That truth has already been emphasised in a previous study, and we need to remember its penetration. God sees the attitude as well as the action. He requires 'truth in the inward parts' (Psalm 51:6).

It is interesting to note that the word 'sight' used in the phrase 'in the sight of the Lord', is translated in The Amplified Bible by the word 'presence' – and that helps to give us its precise impact. We are to humble ourselves in the *presence* of the Lord. The supreme motive for humility, for holiness of life, for obedience, and for all the virtues and graces that we find scattered throughout the scripture, lies not so much in God's knowledge, but in His character; not so much in the fact that God knows what we are doing, but that God Himself is there with us while we are doing it!

People have sometimes written about 'practising the presence of God' and perhaps other Christians have dismissed the phrase as being rather too pietistic to be of practical value. Yet surely there is a sense in which we can say that there is nothing more practical in all the world than practising the presence of God. Perhaps we can only begin to get a grasp of this if we think of God in human terms, in other words, if we think of the Person of the Lord Jesus Christ. Now let me apply this to your own heart and life, even as you read these words. Let me paraphrase and personalise James's command – 'Humble yourselves in the presence of the Lord Jesus Christ' – not *as if* you were in His presence, nor *when* you are in His presence, but *because you are!* Now begin to draft that into every detail of your life. Practise the presence of Jesus in your home. Recognise His presence as you switch on the television set, when you gather around the table in conversation, when you open the pages of a book, when you speak about that person who is absent. Take the same principle into your relationship with husband or wife, your parents or children. Remember that He is there when you speak and think and act in relationship to them. Take it into your business life, into the way you do your work day by day. He is there! He is there when you sit at the desk, when you pick up the telephone, when you start tapping those typewriter keys, when you dictate that letter, drive that lorry, handle those goods. He is there when you deal with your employees; He is there when you react to your employers. Take the same principle into the matter of your Christian service. He sits with you in the Bible class; He is alongside you when you teach those Sunday school children; He is there when you walk up the pulpit steps. He sits with you at those committee meetings; He is there when you cast your vote. Can you possibly escape the impact of what James is saying? Are you proud in His presence? Do you ever strut around with an air of authority and importance – when all the time *He* is there?

The whole issue is so serious, so searching, that perhaps I should add a word of warning. To some people there is

a danger that to dwell on the Lord's actual presence with
us every moment of every day can be so overwhelming that
it could almost be depressing, demoralising, frightening.
The knowledge of their own weakness, and their frequent
failures could tend to drive them to despair. To such people,
let me say that exactly the reverse should be the case! The
sense of the Lord's presence should bring glory, not gloom.
As John so beautifully puts it, 'Then were the disciples glad,
when they saw the Lord'! (John 20:20). David, too, was a
man conscious of his own personal sin and failure, but listen
to the way in which he expressed his feelings when he medi-
tated on the Lord's presence with him – 'This is too glorious,
too wonderful to believe! I can never be lost to your Spirit!
I can never get away from my God! If I go up to heaven, you
are there; if I go down to the place of the dead, you are
there. If I ride the morning winds to the farthest oceans, even
there your hand will guide me, your strength will support
me' (Psalm 139:6–10 The Living Bible). David did not despair at the Lord's presence with him, he delighted in it! That
positive note takes us on to the second part of this verse
about humility, and from how the principle is stressed to

2. *HOW THE PROMISE IS STATED* – 'and He shall lift
you up'.

James crystallises the promise into six words, yet by
examining them carefully we find that it is put in four
different ways.

(1) *In provisional terms* – '*and* He shall lift you up'. This
is the link with the first part of the verse, and reminds us
that the promise is conditional. The promise is not indiscriminate. It is only to the humble. Martin Luther once said
'It is God's nature to make something out of nothing, that
is why He cannot make anything out of him who is not yet
nothing'. That is wonderful truth! The reason why so many
people are ineffective in their Christian service is that they
are doing it in the energy of the flesh, for their own glory, in
carnal enthusiasm. If we are going to be something for God,
then we must genuinely and honestly recognise that we ourselves are nothing except by His enabling grace.

(2) *In positive terms* – 'And He *shall* lift you up'. While
it is true that there is no escaping the condition, it is also

true that there is no denying the promise! – 'He *shall* lift
you up'. That is stated so often in the scripture that the
problem is to know where to stop quoting! Here are two
obvious Old Testament examples – 'When men are cast
down, then thou shalt say, There is lifting up; and He shall
save the humble person' (Job 22:29). 'He raises the poor
from the dust, and lifts the needy from the ash-heap, to
make them sit with princes, with the princes of His people'
(Psalm 113:7–8 RSV). When we come to the New Testament it is interesting to notice that there are three specific
occasions when Jesus thrust home this principle in almost
identical terms. Once in the context of salvation, once in
the context of service and once in the context of social life.
Jesus ended the story of the Pharisee and the publican by
saying 'everyone who exalts himself will be humbled, but he
who humbles himself will be exalted' (Luke 18:14 RSV).
In His judgment on the Pharisees for loving the uppermost
rooms at feasts, and the chief seats in the synagogues He
said 'whoever exalts himself will be humbled, and whoever
humbles himself will be exalted' (Matthew 23:12 RSV).
Then, in teaching the wisdom of taking the lowest place
when invited to a social occasion, He added 'For every one
who exalts himself will be humbled, and he who humbles
himself will be exalted' (Luke 14:11 RSV). This is one of
the laws of the kingdom of God – and it is a law guaranteed
in the words of a promise!

(3) *In powerful terms* – 'and *He* shall lift you up'. So
often pride is linked, in practical terms, with attempts to
lift *ourselves* up. The old man is incurably egotistic. We
constantly want to justify or prove ourselves, or to satisfy
or please ourselves. We want to pander to our pride and
exalt ourselves. But there is no need for this pathetic behaviour! There is no need for this straining and striving to
be superior! God is in control of things, and He has promised
to exalt and to lift up those who are meek, and lowly, and
humble. Again, there is no need for the Christian to feel
that he must resort to worldly behaviour, attitudes and
standards in order to 'get somewhere' in life, or to gain
pleasure or satisfaction. The Bible specifically contrasts 'the
pleasures of sin for a season' (Hebrews 11:25) by saying

that in God's presence there is 'fullness of joy', and that at
His right hand there are 'pleasures for evermore' (Psalm
16:11). Let us leave the 'lifting up' to the Lord! Our duty
is to walk with Him and before our fellow men in a true
spirit of humility, and self-effacement.

(4) *In practical terms* – 'and He shall *lift you up*'. These
words would seem to apply in two senses:–

Firstly, there is a blessing at present – that is to say in
this life. There is blessing in this life promised to those who
walk humbly with their God. Sometimes that blessing is
conscious and simultaneous. Paul, for instance, says 'When
I am weak, then am I strong' (2 Corinthians 12:10). His real
strength coincided with a consciousness of his weakness.
'When people see that I am an ordinary person, then they
see that I have an extraordinary God, and that He em-
powers me'. That is the spirit of what he is saying. The two
go together; they are simultaneous. At other times the real
outworking of the promise is largely unknown to us. But it
does come! It must! God's lifting up follows our casting
down. It is one of the self-governing principles of the grace
of God. Someone has said 'God's mercy seeks the guilty, His
power the weak, His wisdom the ignorant, and His love the
lost'. To those great truths we could add 'and God's grace
seeks the humble'. Just as the water in a river is constantly
seeking to pour itself into the lowest part of the earth that is
accessible to it, so God's grace is constantly poured into the
lowly heart. We need to be lowly to receive the blessing. And
what a blessing it is! The Amplified Bible adds the phrase
'He will lift you up and make your lives significant'. That is
a wonderful phrase! Your life will be made significant to
yourself, significant to others, and we can dare to say, significant to God. Your life will count for God if you will only
humble yourself in His sight.

Secondly, there is a blessing in prospect – that is to say,
in the future life. Matthew Henry once wrote 'The highest
honour in heaven will be the reward of the greatest humility
on earth'. We have the perfect illustration of that in Paul's
letter to the Philippians, where he says, 'Let this mind be in
you, which was also in Christ Jesus: who, being in the form
of God, thought it not robbery to be equal with God: but

made Himself of no reputation, and took upon Him the form
of a servant, and was made in the likeness of men: and being
found in fashion as a man, He humbled Himself, and became
obedient unto death, even the death of the cross. Wherefore
God also hath highly exalted Him, and given Him a name
which is above every name: that at the name of Jesus every
knee should bow, of things in heaven, and things in earth,
and things under the earth; and that every tongue should confess that Jesus Christ is Lord, to the glory of God the
Father' (Philippians 2:5-11). Here is the greatest example of
humility the world has ever seen. Although Jesus was eternally co-equal in the Godhead, He humbled Himself to the
extent of sharing the frailties of human flesh, and even of
passing through the experience of physical and spiritual
death. But that amazing humiliation resulted in supreme
exaltation, giving Him 'a name which is above every name'.
Now just as we cannot match His humility, so we will not
equal His glory. Throughout eternity He will remain the
object of our adoration and praise and worship, but the
Bible clearly teaches that there are degrees of reward and
blessing in heaven. Jesus illustrated this in the parable of the
pounds, in Luke 19, when He spoke of servants given
authority over varying numbers of cities; Paul speaks of a
man being saved and yet also having to 'suffer loss' (1
Corinthians 3:15); and in almost the last verse in the Bible
the Lord says 'And, behold, I come quickly; and my reward
is with me, to give every man according as his work shall be'
(Revelation 22:12).

It is idle to speculate on the detailed meanings of these
statements, but it is important that we should meditate on
the principle they point out so clearly, and then act accordingly, constantly praying for that spirit of humility which
will bring glory to God and blessing to ourselves and to
others, not only here, but in heaven.

Chapter 8

WATCH YOUR LANGUAGE!

'Speak not evil one of another, brethren. He that speaketh evil of his brother, and judgeth his brother, speaketh evil of the law, and judgeth the law: but if thou judge the law, thou art not a doer of the law, but a judge.

There is one lawgiver, who is able to save and to destroy: who art thou that judgest another?'

(James 4:11–12)

As we have already seen in earlier studies, the use of the tongue is one of the major themes in the Epistle of James. In chapter 1 verse 19, for instance, he says 'Wherefore, my beloved brethren, let every man be swift to hear, *slow to speak,* slow to wrath'; and in chapter 2 verse 12, he warns *'So speak ye,* and so do, as they that shall be judged by the law of liberty'; while the opening twelve verses of chapter 3 are all taken up with the same subject, the use of the tongue. Now, in these two verses, he warns his readers yet again of the great dangers involved in sins of speech.

Dr James Moffatt suggests that these two verses should come immediately after chapter 2 verse 13 – but I see no need to transplant them in this way. It is not difficult to make out a case for this being exactly the right spot for these two verses. They come after James has been dealing with the subjects of pride and humility – and the tongue is a major instrument for expressing human pride. How often we justify ourselves by judging others! We lift up our own reputation by lowering the reputation of other people. We promote ourselves by demoting others in what we say. It is very interesting to notice that this was exactly the kind of thing that was condemned by Jesus in the story of the Pharisee and the Publican. Jesus told the story specifically to people who 'trusted in themselves that they were righteous, and despised others' (Luke 18:9). This comes out in the parable where the Pharisee says 'God, I thank Thee, that I am not as other men are, extortioners, unjust, adulterers, or even as this publican. I fast twice in the week. I give tithes of all that I possess'. Notice how the two things went together. He praised himself and derided the other man. For James to follow teaching on pride with another warning about the wrong use of the tongue seems to me to be perfectly natural.

The verses contain one simple commandment, followed by four reasons why it is given, and we shall examine the verses in that order.

1. *THE COMMANDMENT THAT IS URGED* – 'Speak not evil one of another, brethren'.

This phrase could literally be translated 'speak not against one another', and that immediately suggests a very important lesson. So often we say that our words of criticism and condemnation are only against principles, but the truth is that very often they soon involve people, and there is something so sinister in the human heart that, quite frankly, that is often our main intention! How often do we hear somebody criticising the actions taken by someone else, and then adding 'But of course there is nothing personal in this'! All too often, that is a blatant lie. There *is* something personal in it. There is an intention to wound or to weaken. Of course there is no suggestion in this verse that we are prohibited from ever speaking about a brother in Christ, or even from pointing out some error or fault. What is forbidden is to speak evil, or speak against that person. What James is forbidding here is a spirit of negative criticism, a spirit of judgment and condemnation. The phrase he uses apparently carries with it sufficient shades of meaning to include gossip, backbiting and slander as well as the activities of those with what has been called 'a keen sense of rumour'. It is this sort of thing that is so roundly condemned throughout the Bible. The Psalmist says 'Keep your tongue from evil, and your lips from speaking deceit' (Psalm 34:13 RSV). Paul writes 'Let all bitterness, and wrath, and anger, and clamour, and evil speaking, be put away from you, with all malice' (Ephesians 4:31). Again, he writes 'But now ye also put off all these; anger, wrath, malice, blasphemy, filthy communi-

cation out of your mouth' (Colossians 3:8). The Apostle
Peter adds 'Wherefore laying aside all malice, and all guile,
and hypocrisies, and envies, and all evil speakings, as new-
born babes, desire the sincere milk of the world, that ye may
grow thereby' (1 Peter 2:1–2). In passing, notice Peter's
context. He is speaking of someone new-born as a Christian,
and his point surely is that even a young Christian should
see the evil of these things and cut them out. On a human
level, good speech is one of the marks of progress in a child.
We ask a parent 'Is the baby talking yet?' A mother proudly
says 'Little Jennifer began to talk last week'. And the inference is, the baby is making progress. The better baby
talks, the more progress is being made. The same is true for
the Christian!

We have looked at some length, in earlier studies, at
James's words on the misuse of the tongue, and we might
therefore do no more at this point than to emphasise just
one aspect of it, and that is tale-bearing. D. E. Hoste, the
former General Director of the China Inland Mission, once
made this challenging statement – 'Looking back over these
50 years, I really think that if I were asked to mention one
thing that has done more harm, and occasioned more sorrow
and division in God's work than anything else, I should say,
tale-bearing'. How terrible, yet how sadly true! This is surely
one of the scourges of the church, one of the main fertilizers
of even the evangelical grapevine – the passing on of rumour,
of gossip, of stories that are tinged with something a little
unclean, dishonest or critical. We know this so well that
there is no need to elaborate. The important thing is to know
what we should do about it. What should our action be
when we hear such a story about a brother or a sister in
Christ? Well, what would you do if someone passed on to
you a foreign coin, a coin that was of no commercial value,
a coin with which you could not engage in any honest
trade? If you were honest, you would immediately take it
out of circulation. You would not pass it on to someone
else and transfer its uselessness to them. Surely we should
do exactly the same with the kind of thing we have mentioned here? We should take the story or gossip or rumour
out of circulation, by refusing to pass it on!

But perhaps the whole truth lies even deeper. We should not even pass on a true story if it might harm or hurt someone, if it is going to be 'speaking against' a brother or sister in the Lord. That, after all, is doing the devil's work for him. He is described very clearly in the Bible as 'the accuser of our brethren' (Revelation 12:10), and for a Christian deliberately to engage in the passing on of gossip and rumour against another brother or sister in Christ, accusing them, even indirectly, on something which could only cause them harm, is to do the devil's work for him. May the Lord help us to be innocent of such a terrible thing! This is the commandment that is urged.

2. *THE CONSIDERATIONS THAT ARE USED* – 'He that speaketh evil of his brother, and judgeth his brother, speaketh evil of the law, and judgeth the law; but if thou judge the law, thou art not a doer of the law, but a judge. There is one lawgiver, who is able to save and to destroy: who art thou that judgest another?'

James now gives four reasons, or considerations, why we should obey the particular commandment to 'speak not evil one of another'.

(1) *Because of the partnership it spoils.* Notice the way that he appeals to his readers. He uses the word 'brethren' or 'brother' three times in verse 11, and the word 'another' in verse 12 is a word that is translated in the Revised Standard Version, The Amplified Bible and other translations as 'neighbour'. It seems very clear, then, that James is thinking particularly on behaviour within the church, within the fellowship, and he appeals to their relationship as brethren as a reason for not engaging in malicious tale-bearing. Here surely is a word for today. I am sure that as a whole we sit too lightly to the wonderful relationship that binds us together as Christians. We have paid too little attention to the wonderful things the Bible says about our relationship to each other, and the result is that we miss the real essence of the kind of appeal made by James at this point, this particular consideration that he urges in backing up his command. My experience has convinced me that the effect of that error is worldwide. Within churches, committees, councils, fellowships and Christian groups of every kind there is

a disgraceful amount of evil speaking one of another. And the result? Often, things seem to go on very much as before. Outwardly, there seems to be unity. The work plods on. There is apparently a measure of blessing. But the partnership is not *real*. The fellowship has been marred. What a need there is for honest confession and wholehearted forgiveness in this whole area of Christian relationships! It is interesting to see how, in a different context, when Paul appeals to believers to do nothing that would offend another Christian, he refers to him as 'thy brother . . . one for whom Christ died' (Romans 14:15 RSV). That serves to emphasise in an even more vivid way the reality of our relationship to each other, because it tells us that it was forged at Calvary. We are blood brothers – and the blood is the blood of Christ. What a tragedy when that wonderful relationship is spoilt by criticism, backbiting or rumour!

(2) *Because of the principle it smashes*. '. . . He that speaketh evil of his brother, and judgeth his brother, speaketh evil of the law, and judgeth the law'. What does James mean by 'the law', and in what way does criticism and rumour-mongering 'speak evil' of it and 'judge' it? The straightforward answer would seem to be that 'the law' is God's law in general, but in particular that part of the law that deals with our personal relationships. James himself earlier called it 'the royal law' (chapter 2 verse 8) and had reminded his readers that it could be summed up in these words – 'Thou shalt love thy neighbour as thyself'. This of course was carrying over into the New Testament the commandment given in the Old, 'You shall not take vengeance or bear any grudge against the sons of your own people, but you shall love your neighbour as yourself: I am the Lord' (Leviticus 19:18 RSV). Jesus summed up the last six commandments in the decalogue in one phrase, 'You shall love your neighbour as yourself' (Mark 12:31 RSV), while the Apostle Paul added 'For the whole law is fulfilled in one word, "You shall love your neighbour as yourself" ' (Galatians 5:14 RSV).

Do you see the point that is being made here? To love is to act in a way deliberately calculated to be for the blessing of the person towards whom you act. Speaking evil, on the other hand, is often done from exactly the opposite motives and always results in the opposite effect. In other words, when we speak against someone we smash the principle of acting in love toward them, even when we do so from allegedly good motives.

Here is a simple principle that we must bear very seriously in mind. But notice the particular thing that James says. In smashing its principle you 'speak evil of the law' itself. You judge it. In other words, you know it is there, you know what it says, but you deliberately set it on one side and carry out the things you want to do. Surely this is nothing less than Christian permissiveness. It is saying 'The law has some value, but my own personal judgment of the situation comes first'. But the biblical requirement is that we do *not* smash the principle of love, but rather that we guard it, uphold it, foster it. As Paul puts it, 'Let every one of us please his neighbour for his good to edification' (Romans 15:2). Notice how precisely that wording is to the point we are discussing. We are to *please* our neighbours for their *good* to *edification*. We are to act towards them for their benefit, for their building up – in other words we are to act in love. Paul repeats the same truth in another Epistle, and interestingly enough he specifically links it to the use of the tongue – 'Let no corrupt communication proceed out of your mouth, but that which is good to the use of edifying, that it may minister grace unto the hearers' (Ephesians 4:29). When we behave like that, we uphold the great principle of loving our neighbour as ourselves. When we use our tongues in slanderous, back-biting, tale-bearing activities, then we are smashing that principle.

(3) *Because of the prerogative it seizes* – 'but if Thou judge the law, thou art not a doer of the law, but a judge. There is one lawgiver, who is able to save and to destroy'. James now takes the issue even further. Not only does a person who behaves in the way we have mentioned break the law, but in doing so he judges it. In other words, he puts it in its place. He decides how far it will apply to him. Either that or he says in effect that it is unimportant, or unnecessary. Either way he is a judge of the law. Think that through very carefully! It is a thunderous argument. Who can possibly

deny that it is true? God's law is not given for our approval, nor for our opinions, nor even as a general guide. It is given to us for our unqualified and immediate obedience, and as soon as we do other than that we are at fault, not least by becoming judges of the law. This directly opposes James's great concern throughout the whole epistle, which is that we should be 'doers of the word, and not hearers only' (1:22).

But James is not finished! He says 'There is one lawgiver, who is able to save and to destroy'. Most translations insert the words 'and judge' after the word 'lawgiver'. The meaning is obviously not 'there are many lawgivers and judges but only one is able to save and to destroy'. The real sense comes out well in the Revised Standard Version which translates it 'there is one lawgiver and judge, he who is able to save and to destroy'. The reference is quite clearly to God, and it would be immediately recognised by James's readers.

We have an illustration of this in the story of Naaman in 2 Kings 5. You will remember that the king of Syria sent Naaman to the king of Israel, asking him to ensure that Naaman was healed of his leprosy. When that message reached the king of Israel he was terrified and cried out 'Am I God to kill and to make alive . . . ?' (2 Kings 5:7). He recognised immediately that that kind of thing was God's prerogative. Of course there are many scriptures which tell us that God is a lawgiver or a judge and both titles are combined in this cry from the prophet — 'For the Lord is our judge, the Lord is our lawgiver, the Lord is our king; he will save us' (Isaiah 33:22).

But why does James bring in this argument? Why take us to God as lawgiver and judge at this point? There seem to me to be at least two reasons why he should do so, and those are two qualifications that belong to God alone.

Firstly, authority – 'There is one lawgiver', or, if we accepted some other translations, 'one lawgiver and judge'. Now that is obviously true, yet under this one Divine authority there are many others. There are kings and rulers, presidents and ministers, public officers of many kinds. All exercise authority over others. So do employers, teachers, parents and many others – and even to those our right

attitude is one of submission and obedience. As the Apostle
Paul says 'Put them in mind to be subject to principalities
and powers, to obey magistrates, to be ready to every good
work. To speak evil of no man, to be no brawlers, but
gentle, shewing all meekness unto all men' (Titus 3:1). Now
if it is an immediately recognised fact that we ought to be
submissive and obedient to these earthly rulers and authorities, how much more should we be submissive and obedient
to God and to His law, not seizing His prerogative by adjust-
ing the law to our own personal judgments and convenience?
We saw this earlier, in our study of chapter 4 verse 7. God
has ultimate authority.

Secondly, ability – James says that God 'is able to save
and to destroy'. This is not only true physically but spiritually. The eternal destinies of all men are in the hands of
God, and his judgment in every case will be true and
righteous, perfect and flawless. That being so, we can safely
leave with Him the smaller issues of everyday life! This is
the real point James is making here. Notice how Paul brings
this out – 'Beloved, never avenge yourselves, but leave it to
the wrath of God; for it is written, "Vengeance is mine, I
will repay, says the Lord"' (Romans 12:19 RSV). It seems
to me that so often our criticism in particular seems to be
born of a nervous conviction that we are the only people who
can possibly put the world straight. When will we learn to
behave in this area of life in a way that confirms our faith
that God is in control, and is working all things according
to the counsel of His will? He is 'able both to save and to
destroy'. Linking this in with something we noticed a little
earlier, it is not only a sad thing when Christians do the
devil's work for him – it is even sadder when Christians try
to do God's work for *Him!* Let us not seize His prerogative.

(4) *Because of the presumption it shows* – '. . . who art
thou that judgest another?' What an exquisite use of sanc-
tified sarcasm! The Amplified Bible translates the phrase
'But you, who are you to pass judgment on your neighbour?'
There is an obvious link by contrast here with the first part
of the verse. God has the authority and the ability to give
laws, to judge, to save, to destroy. 'Now', says James, 'God
has that authority and ability – do you?' In fact, James is

so sure of his argument that he can limit it to just one thing – the question of judging our fellow-men. James gives no specific reasons why we are not able to do so (other than the implied contrast I have mentioned), but if we are humble and honest enough, they are easily found. In contrast to the two divine qualifications we saw for God as a lawgiver and judge, here are two obvious disqualifications from which we all suffer, and which should prevent us from judging one another.

Firstly, our lack of perfect information. It has been said that 'to know all is to forgive all'. I for one have certainly been guilty on occasion of criticising someone, and then had to reverse my opinion of the situation when I heard the other side of the story. Even a High Court Judge, with hundreds of pages of written evidence before Him, can be misled because of false or incomplete evidence. There have been classic cases of miscarriage of justice, when other factors came to light after the verdict was given and sometimes after the penalty was irreversibly paid. We run the same kind of risk when we pass hasty judgments on the basis of our limited knowledge. Paul has a word that exactly meets the point here – 'Therefore judge nothing before the time, until the Lord come, who both will bring to light the hidden things of darkness, and will make manifest the counsels of the hearts' (1 Corinthians 4:5).

Secondly, our lack of personal integrity. Here is the second thing that disqualifies us from judging others – we ourselves are guilty people! The Bible gives a vivid illustration of this in the case of the woman taken in adultery. The crowd gathered eagerly around her, ready to stone her to death for her sin, but when Jesus said 'He that is without sin among you, let him first cast a stone at her' we read that 'being convicted by their own conscience' they 'went out one by one' (John 8:7–9). They recognised that they were disqualified by their own lack of integrity! In his book 'Make Your Faith Work', Dr Louis H. Evans asks 'Is there that blamelessness in us, that purity of motive, that perfection, that overflowing charity, that love of the sinner that makes us like Christ and so qualifies us for unprejudiced judgment? James challenges us to a sense of humility in this whole area'. Jesus drove home the same challenge in the Sermon on the Mount, when He spoke of a man taking critical notice of a speck of dust in someone else's eye while a plank of wood was sticking out of his own. To set oneself up as a universal critic of the actions and attitudes and lives of other people is to show the most arrogant presumption and to fail completely to recognise one's lack of qualification to do so. As somebody once very cleverly put it 'The critic who starts with himself will have no time to take on outside contracts'. If we do judge one another, if we do take it upon ourselves to speak against one another, it shows an unhealthy presumption for the truth is that we are not qualified to do so. In the plain, simple language of the Word of God 'Let us not therefore judge one another any more' (Romans 14:13). To obey that commandment wholeheartedly, unreservedly and continually, would move many people into a whole new dimension of Christian living and relationship with their brothers and sisters in Christ.

These verses have been necessary, but negative. They have told us what *not* to do. These words by James Whitcomb Riley will help us to grasp the other, obvious side of the truth that James has been teaching –

> When over the fair frame or friend or foe
> The shadow of disgrace shall fall; instead
> Of words of blame, or proof of so and so,
> Let something good be said!
>
> No generous heart may vainly turn aside
> In ways of sympathy; no soul so dead
> But may awaken strong and glorified,
> If something good be said.
>
> And so I charge thee, by the thorny crown,
> And by the Cross on which the Saviour bled,
> And by our own soul's hope for fair renown;
> Let something good be said!

Chapter 9

D.V.

'Go now, ye that say, Today or tomorrow we will go into such a city, and continue there a year, and buy and sell, and get gain:

Whereas ye know not what shall be on the morrow. For what is your life? It is even a vapour, that appeareth for a little time, and then vanisheth away.

For that ye ought to say, If the Lord will, we shall live, and do this, or that.

But now ye rejoice in your boastings: all such rejoicing is evil'. (James 4:13–16)

It is sometimes possible to get the impression, on a superficial reading of his epistle, that James is jumping from one subject to another, with no apparent reason. The Epistle of James has been described as a picture gallery – and of course in a picture gallery no two subjects may ever come together. But what I have increasingly discovered is that the closer you look at this letter, the more you see the integration there is between sections that appear to be totally disassociated. This is not to say that it is illegitimate for James to deal briefly with one subject and then pass onto another which is not in any way related to it – but as we have already seen, there is a connection between many of the sections that we initially might feel are not in any way linked at all. I think we have an example here.

Verses 11 and 12 had to do with judging other people, with back-biting, criticism and rumour-mongering. The verses now before us seem to deal in their original impact with businessmen planning their diaries – and there does not seem to be any obvious connection there! But there is one: the deadly sin of *pride*. In the case of the people dealt with in verses 11 and 12, that pride enabled them to pronounce on the lives of others. In this case their pride enabled them to presume upon their own life. In the previous verses James

dealt with pride in judging other people; now, he is going to
isolate another out-working of pride and use a very well-
known daily experience to illustrate it. First of all, we see.
1. *THE ARROGANCE HE CONDEMNS* – 'Go to now,
ye that say, Today or tomorrow we will go into such a city,
and buy and sell, and get gain: . . . But now ye rejoice in
your boastings: all such rejoicing is evil' (vv. 13 and 16).

The Jewish penchant for business is well-known the world
over, and James undoubtedly had businessmen in mind here.
But not all businessmen. He is not condemning industry and
commerce out of hand. The Bible never condemns out of
hand honest initiative, hard work, or the accumulation of
wealth. James has only *certain* businessmen in mind, and
isolates them with the phrase beginning with the words 'ye
that say'. We can safely assume that the words, 'ye that
say' refer to spirit as well as speech. These words were outward signs of their whole attitude to life, and that attitude
was one of total arrogance. They strutted around as if they
owned the place! The idea of failure, the thought that their
plans might come unstuck, never entered their heads. They
acted as if nothing could possibly come between them and
the schemes they had worked out for the future. Notice the
number of things that filled their minds.

(1) *The plan* – 'Today or tomorrow'. Perhaps we would
better translate the words 'today and tomorrow' but in either
case it was clear that they had a plan in mind. They were
looking into the future and making specific plans as to what
was going to happen. As the father of a large family, I have
often listened to my children excitedly discussing some
future event, such as a family holiday. As the day drew
near, so they would get more and more enthusiastic about
all the wonderful things they were going to do, and any
thought that their plans might come unstuck would never
once enter their young heads. But the people to whom James
was referring were not children, they were mature men, they
were men of the world, men used to what are called the
changes and chances of everyday life. They must have
experienced ups and downs in the past, they must have
known failure, frustration and disappointment at times,
and yet they went blithely on, planning their future without

any thought that the plans might not materialise. Like those described in Isaiah 56:12, they said 'tomorrow shall be as this day, and much more abundant'. That was the plan. Then notice

(2) *The place* – 'we will go into such a city', or, as the Amplified Bible puts it, 'we will go into such and such a city'. With a little imagination we can see them with a map spread out over the desk, discussing density of population, trade routes and other relevant factors before choosing a city for their next business venture. I remember once travelling by train from London to the West Country, and five or six businessmen, obviously area representatives for some big concern or other, sat at the table next to me. By any assessment they were worldly men and, of course, I hardly expected them to get their Authorised Versions out and begin a Bible study! – but what struck me so forcibly was that their conversation was so proud, so arrogant. They spoke as if they ruled their particular world. They spoke about future plans and projects, decided exactly what was going to happen, how much money was going to be made, what developments would follow, and so on. It all left me very sad at heart, because there was an attitude of such monumental arrogance about it all. That is the kind of thing that James is getting at here. Then next we see

(3) *The period* – 'and continue there a year'. As we shall see later, these men had no guarantee of tomorrow, but there they were confidently forecasting twelve months ahead. They said, 'We are going into such and such a place, and we are going to stay there for a whole year'. The idea that their lives might be cut short in six months, or that there might be an economic recession, or that there might be some other contingency upsetting their plans never seems to have entered their minds. When James uses the word 'year', he is not necessarily thinking of an exact period of 365 days. It is just a picture that represents a principle, and the principle is that these men were acting as if the whole of the future was so secure that they could plan it without any fear of failure. It is true that we have all the time in the world, but these people were acting as if their world had plenty of time. There is a vast difference! We do have all the time in the world,

but can you tell me how much time the world has? That is the important thing. Incidentally, when people say 'I just haven't time to do that' or 'If only I had more time', there is a sense in which those are fatuous remarks because we have all the time in the world. Those who achieve most in the world, those with a staggering output and productivity, have exactly the same amount of time as the man who achieves little. The difference is in the way they use it. Next, there was

(4) *The programme* – 'buy and sell'. Notice again how much was being arrogantly taken for granted. In effect, they were saying 'we will have the money to buy, we will have the goods to sell, we will have customers to charge'. All of these things were taken for granted. 'We are going there, and we will buy and sell. Whether we have been there before or not, whether we are known, or unknown in the place; these things are immaterial. Just leave it to us. Everything is going to be fine'. That was their whole attitude. But there is something else to notice, and that is that now, mingled with God being left out, (which is the real tragedy of the opening comments), self is being brought in. 'We will go . . . we will continue . . .'; the mark of all this is that God is being left out, there is no reference to God. Now, another element comes to light – 'we will buy and sell'. Here is a plain illustration of a biblical law, and that is that to the extent to which God is left out, self is brought in. To the extent that God is pushed to the circumference of our lives, self is brought into the centre. To put it the other way round – to the extent to which God is enthroned, self is dethroned. John put it in one terse phrase 'He must increase, but I must decrease' (John 3:3a). If we make something of ourselves, then God is shadowed in the situation, and people are not able to see Him clearly. If we make much of the Lord, then we must decrease. If we magnify the Lord, then we are hidden. The important thing is not that people should say to us 'What a wonderful person he is' but 'What a wonderful Saviour he has'! These businessmen left God out and brought themselves right into the centre of the picture – 'we will buy and sell'. Now we are getting to the real heart of the truth, because after the programme, come

(5) *The profits* – 'and get gain'. Here was the whole object

of the exercise! It began with 'today and tomorrow'; it went on to 'such a city'; it was to last 'a year'; in that time they would 'buy and sell' – but now we discover what it is all about, 'we will get gain'. The word 'gain' is apparently a word that includes a passion for making money. It was not just a question of making prudent business arrangements, it was a passion for making money. This was the only, or major object of the whole venture.

Peter speaks of those with 'hearts trained in greed' (2 Peter 2:14 RSV), and it is the same spirit that James is attacking here. Here were people always at the stretch for every penny of profit that could be made. Not only was God left out, but self was brought in until it filled the whole picture. And, as ever, James has drawn his picture very true to life!

Life with God left out. Have you ever thought that that describes most of the people living in our country today? God is left out. In other words, they are what I call practical atheists. Let me illustrate what I mean. Some time ago, I was speaking to several hundred schoolchildren. They were unusually restless and inattentive, and in an attempt to get their attention, I suddenly asked them an apparently ridiculous question – 'Have you ever seen a pig saying grace before a meal'? There was a short burst of laughter, and then a puzzled silence. 'Well', I went on 'what is your answer to the question? Give me the answer all together'. Needless to say, there was a universal roar of 'No!' 'Now', I went on quickly, 'Let me ask you another question. Do *you* say grace before meals'. There was no laughter this time, just silence, which I broke by saying 'Would you now answer that question all together'. Again it seemed that everyone in the building shouted out the same word – 'No!' 'Thank you', I replied, 'That is of great help to me. You see, I have never been to this school before, and I had no idea what kind of people you were. Now I know – you are on the same level as the pigs!' Shock tactics, if you like! – but they worked, and from then on I had a close hearing, perhaps for the simple reasons that, however reluctantly, those young people realised that what I had said was true. They were living each day with no reference whatever to God. In that sense, they were living like animals. They got up in the morning, they washed (presumably!), took their meals, felt the sunshine and the rain, breathed the fresh air, enjoyed the company of those they knew, went home at the end of the day, closed their eyes in sleep – and left God clean out of their thinking. Life with God left out! In our dealings with the world, in our concern for the lost, in our prayers for our unbelieving friends, we need to recognise that that is the deliberate experience of many people.

James sums it all up in verse 16 – 'But now ye rejoice in your boastings: all such rejoicing is evil'. The Amplified Bible puts it like this – 'But as it is, you boast falsely in your presumption and self-conceit. All such boasting is wrong'. These men may have been moral, honest and hard working, yet they were condemned for this one thing – they were self-concerned, self-centred and self-conceited. They left God out of the reckoning. They got so caught up in their business they had no time for the Bible. They were so concerned when they went to a new town to ask where the market was, that they forgot to ask where the church was. They were so busy making profit they had no time to go to prayer. What was even worse was that they boasted in their arrogance. James's verdict is blunt and straightforward – 'All your boasting is wrong' – and its wrongness was rooted in God being left out.

The Old Testament gives us a classic warning of this danger, in a word spoken by the Lord, through Moses, to the people of Israel – 'Take heed lest you forget the Lord your God, by not keeping his commandments and His ordinances and His statutes, which I command you this day: lest, when you have eaten and are full, and have built goodly houses and live in them, and when your herds and flocks multiply, and your silver and gold is multiplied, and all that you have is multiplied, then your heart be lifted up, and you forget the Lord your God, who brought you out of the land of Egypt, out of the house of bondage, who led you through the great and terrible wilderness, with its fiery serpents and scorpions and thirsty ground where there was no water, who brought you water out of the flinty rock, who fed you in the wilderness with manna which your fathers did not know, that He might humble you and test you, to do you good in the end. Beware lest you say in your heart, "My power and the might of my hand have gotten me this wealth" ' (Deuteronomy 8 : 11–17 RSV).

The Bible's warning is clear : when things are going well, beware lest you forget God! It is said that when Napoleon Bonaparte was considering invading Russia, a friend tried to dissuade him, saying 'Man proposes, but God disposes'. Bonaparte's reply was 'I dispose as well as propose'. A Christian who heard of this said, 'I set that down as the turning point of Bonaparte's fortunes. God will not suffer a creature with impunity thus to usurp His prerogative'. As all the world knows, that forecast was absolutely true. The Russian campaign marked the beginning of Napoleon's downfall. Man proposes, but God disposes. For us to go through life, or to conduct any part of our lives, without reference to God, smacks of arrogance – and arrogance is something that the Bible everywhere, and not least in the Epistle of James, condemns outright. So much, then, for the first thing, the arrogance he condemns. Now we turn to

2. *THE ATTITUDE HE COMMENDS* – 'Whereas ye know not what shall be on the morrow. For what is your life? It is even a vapour, that appeareth for a little time, and then vanisheth away. For that ye ought to say, If the Lord will, we shall live, and do this, or that'. (vv. 14–15).

Having exposed their arrogance as evil, James points to the right attitude they ought to adopt. The directive, the instruction that he gives them, is contained in verse 15, but as that is based on verse 14, they can both be taken together. First of all, notice

(1) *The principle they ought to remember* – 'Whereas ye know not what shall be on the morrow. For what is your life? It is even a vapour, that appeareth for a little time, and then vanisheth away'. (v. 14).

The principle they seemed to be forgetting altogether was the brevity of life. They said 'We will'; God said 'Ye know not'. They planned for a year; God said they were not even certain of tomorrow. They thought they were independent; God said they were ignorant – 'Ye know not'. That, of course, is the plain, straightforward teaching of scripture in so many places. In the book of Proverbs, for instance, we read 'Do not boast about tomorrow, for you do not know what a day may bring forth'. (Proverbs 27:1 RSV) Notice how precisely the brevity of life is directly linked to the matter of boasting. Not only do men plan without God – that is the central point – but they actually boast about it, they make arrogant plans leaving God right out of the picture.

Then notice how James presses the point home. 'For what is your life?' That is an appeal to reason. He begins the section with the words, 'Go to now, ye that say' in verse 13. The words 'Go to now' would be better translated 'come now'. It reminds us of that other appeal to reason – ' "Come now, let us reason together", says the Lord' (Isaiah 1:18 RSV). We have a reasonable God, a reasonable faith, and so James makes his appeal to reason and says, in effect, 'Come now, you who are making these grandiose plans with no reference to God. What is your life? Have you ever stopped for a moment to think that you might be cut off in the middle of all your plans? It is not only evil, it is downright foolish to make these plans with no reference to God whatsoever'. The answer to James's question 'What is your life' is so obvious that he does not even invite a nanswer, he gives it himself. He says, 'What is your life? It is even a vapour, that appeareth for a little time and then vanisheth away', That principle, too, is woven into the very fabric of the Holy Scriptures. Notice the Bible's insistence on this solemn truth – 'Our days on the earth are like a shadow' (1 Chronicles 29:15 RSV); 'My days are swifter than a weaver's shuttle' (Job 7:6 RSV); 'My life is a breath' (Job 7:7 RSV); 'My days are swifter than a runner' (Job 9:24 RSV); 'Behold, thou hast made my days a few hand breadths' (Psalm 39:5 RSV); 'My days pass away like smoke' (Psalm 102:3 RSV); 'My days are like an evening shadow; I wither away like grass' (Psalm 102:11 RSV); 'My dwelling is plucked up and removed from me like a shepherd's tent' (Isaiah 38:12 RSV); 'All flesh is like grass and all its glory like the flower of grass' (1 Peter 1:24).

Here, then, is a plain, straightforward appeal to reason. Life is brief and even in a civilised and well medicated society like the one in which we live, it still remains remarkably true that threescore years and ten is something like the average span of life, with nearly a third of it gone by the time we reach the end of our teens.

Yet even that is not the whole point that James is making here. The words 'it is a vapour' are perhaps not the best translation of the original, and we need to turn to several other versions to get at the deeper truth. The Revised Version, for instance, has 'ye are a vapour'; and the Revised Standard Version says, 'you are a mist'; while the 20th Century New Testament reads 'you are but a mist'. Several other translations have similar wordings, and the point they emphasise is this: the principle that James is making is not a philosophical one, but a personal one. He is not talking about life in general, but about people in particular. In plain language, *you* are a mist, *you* are a vapour, *you* are like a smoke. The moment you were born you began to die, and that moment of death could come at any time, by design, by disease, by decay or by disaster. We hold on to the precious tenancy of life without so much as a moment's notice to quit being due to us. We are not here to stay, we are here to go. We should reckon seriously with that!

The man in Luke 12 had a problem. Business was going so well that he was pressed for storage space for his harvest. He decided to pull down his barns, build bigger ones, get his bumper crop safely in, and then 'eat, drink and be merry'. That one harvest would see him through for 'many years'. But he had forgotten the brevity of life – 'But God said to him, "Fool! This night your soul is required of you" '. Here was a man of similar spirit to the men to whom James was speaking. He was so wrapped up in business that he forgot that life has a spiritual dimension. He was so busy with his accounts that he forgot he was accountable!

Remember this principle – life is not meant for self or for earthly treasure. It is meant for God, for heaven, for holiness; and because it is so brief, so uncertain, so fragile, we should apply ourselves first and foremost to those issues and 'seek . . . first the kingdom of God and his righteousness' (Matthew 6:33). We should pray with the Psalmist 'So teach us to number our days that we may get a heart of

wisdom' (Psalm 90:12 RSV). From the principle they ought
to remember, James now turns to

(2) *The Providence they ought to recognise* – 'For that ye
ought to say, If the Lord will, we shall live, and do this, or
that'.

The central point of their folly was that they left God
out of the reckoning. Notice how concisely James now puts
God right back in the centre of things, or, rather, how he
shows that God ought to overshadow every situation. He
says that their attitude ought to be '*If* the Lord will, we
shall'. James was not advising them to sit back and do
nothing. What was being condemned was not their business,
but their boasting; not their industry, but their independence;
not their acumen, but their arrogance. There was no
reference to God in their planning, and no room for Him in
their programme. Someone has said 'The essence of sin is
arrogance, and the essence of salvation is submission'. This
truth reaches out into the whole of life. James says that the
right attitude to life is to recognise the providence, or
sovereignty of God, in other words to recognise that God
controls it all in every detail.

There are two things about this attitude that will help us
to hold James's point in perspective here –

Firstly, it is biblical. That would be true if this was the
only reference to the sovereignty of God in the whole Bible,
but in fact this truth is woven throughout the whole of scripture. Perhaps the clearest verse of all is where Paul states
plainly that God 'accomplishes all things according to the
counsel of His will' (Ephesians 1:11 RSV). In other words,
there are no accidents with God, no unforeseen circumstances. Nothing takes God by surprise. God has a plan, not only
for the world in general, but for lives in particular. It is wonderful for Christians to recognise this! Paul speaks of 'good
works, which God prepared beforehand, that we should walk
in them' (Ephesians 2:10 RSV), and the writer to the
Hebrews speaks of life as 'the race that is set before us'
(Hebrews 12:1). God *does* have things mapped out, and the
Bible not only states it in principle and doctrine, but by
example, too. Take the Apostle Paul. If ever there was a
man who was dynamic and explosive and a man of drive,

decision, and initiative, then he was that man. Now listen to him discussing his plans! 'I will return again unto you', he tells the Christians at Ephesus, *'if God will'* (Acts 18:21). He writes to the church at Rome that he has been praying that he might have 'a prosperous journey *by the will of God*, to come unto you' (Romans 1:10). To the Christians at Corinth he writes 'I will come to you shortly, *if the Lord will'* (1 Corinthians 4:19); and again 'I trust to tarry a while with you, *if the Lord permit'* (1 Corinthians 16:7). This dynamic man recognised that all of his hopes and plans and aspirations and visions and enthusiasms were to be stamped 'DV'. Deo Volente! If the Lord will! Not only is this truth biblical, but

Secondly, it is beneficial. Surely that is obvious! Here is the perfect answer to the fretting, and fuming, and worrying and frenetic scrambling of our 20th Century. Jesus said '. . . do not be anxious about tomorrow' (Matthew 6:34 RSV); Paul added 'Have no anxiety about anything' (Philippians 4:6 RSV); and those demands become reasonable demands when we recognise that there is no point in us being anxious about the future, because the future is in God's hands. While we do not know what the future holds, we do know Who holds the future – a sovereign God of wonderful love and infinite and specific care for His people. To grasp this is to steer clear of two great dangers in this area. One is the danger of planning recklessly without reference to God, and the other is the danger of living life carelessly and aimlessly in the hope that God will work it all out somehow or another. Planning for the future is both wise and scriptural, but we must plan prayerfully. It is not enough to make our plans first and then ask God to bless them. The right attitude is first of all to seek God's will before we make our plans, and then only to make them when we feel happy in our heart that we are in the will of God. As John puts it 'If our hearts do not condemn us, we have confidence before God' (1 John 3:21 RSV). Paul's first prayer as a Christian on the Damascus Road was, 'Lord what wilt thou have me to do?' (Acts 9:6), and that is a prayer that fully incorporates God's sovereignty and man's responsibility. Commenting on these verses in his book 'The Tests of Faith', the Rev.

J. Alec Motyer writes, 'He (James) would have us empty
our lives of proud planning which does not fear and bow to
the will of God and submit all things to His ordering hand'.
W. F. Lloyd made the issue both personal and positive in
the words of his hymn –

> *My times are in Thy hand,*
> *My God, I wish them there;*
> *My life, my friends, my soul I leave*
> *Entirely to Thy care.*

> *My times are in Thy hand,*
> *Whatever there may be,*
> *Pleasing or painful, dark or bright,*
> *As best may seem to Thee.*

> *My times are in Thy hand*
> *Why should I doubt or fear?*
> *A Father's hand will never cause*
> *His child a needless tear.*

> *My times are in Thy hand,*
> *Jesus the crucified;*
> *The Hand my cruel sins had pierced*
> *Is now my guard and guide.*

> *My times are in Thy hand;*
> *I'll always trust in Thee,*
> *And after death at Thy right hand*
> *I shall for ever be.*

Chapter 10

KNOWING AND DOING

'Therefore to him that knoweth to do good, and doeth it not, to him it is sin'.   (James 4:17)

To the casual reader, this verse looks to be no more than an appendix to the chapter. Some might even go further and say that, like a physical appendix, it serves no useful purpose and could be removed without loss. But the truth is exactly the opposite. In fact, I have come to the conclusion that it is one of the most penetrating verses in the whole of the Epistle. The basic lesson, of course, hardly needs any comment at all, it lies there right on the surface. If you know that a thing is right, but you do not do it, then for you, that is sin, the sin of omitting to do right. Much more, however, lies beneath the surface, as we shall discover. But before going into its detail, have you noticed that this is a very telling and challenging verse in what we could call the 'sinless perfection' issue. It certainly strikes a mortal blow at the extreme viewpoint that says it is possible in this life to live without sin of any kind. Now according to this verse, in order to do that, a man would not only have to avoid doing everything that was sinful, he would *always* have to do *everything* that he knew to be good. It would not merely be a question of avoiding known sin, it would be a question of constantly doing everything that he knew to be good. I will begin to believe that doctrine when I meet someone who can testify to obeying it!

Now let us dig into the truth of the whole verse, and in order to do so, we will do three things.

1. *ESTABLISH THE CONNECTION* – that is, the connection with the verses that have gone before. Some, of course, say that there is no connection at all. Certain liberal commentators say that James picked up this rather nice idea somewhere, had it at the back of his mind, thought it would be interesting to include it somewhere, and dropped it in at

the end of chapter 4. I have always found that kind of exegesis utterly illogical and totally unsatisfying!

The verse begins with a 'Therefore' and we ought therefore to be looking for a connection with what has gone before. As someone once said, 'Whenever you see the word "therefore" in the Bible, ask yourself what it is there for'! That is very sound advice. After all, you do not begin an argument, or a document, or a letter with the word "therefore'. What you do first of all is to state certain facts, and then add the word 'therefore' as a bridge to some kind of application, or comment, or request, or result, or demand that follows from the facts. James uses the word 'therefore' here in just that way – so what is the connection? As we saw in the previous study, verses 13–16 have to do with boastful businessmen who arrogantly planned their lives without any reference to God. They left God out of the reckoning. In his commentary entitled 'The Behaviour of Belief' Spiros Zodhiates says that most translaters have missed the continuity of thought between verse 16 and verse 17 by misunderstanding the meaning of one word. He claims that verse 17 should begin 'Therefore *he* (the merchant) knowing to do good . . .'. This would presumably imply that verse 17 has in mind Christian businessmen who were getting so caught up in their work that they were leaving God right out on the circumference of their lives. In other words, they were practical atheists, as we described them in our last study. They were not intellectual atheists claiming there was no God, they were practical atheists, behaving as if there was none. A backsliding believer can go through a day, a week, a month or even a year or more, and for all practical purposes, the drift of his life is atheistic – other, perhaps, than attendance at some religious gatherings. Perhaps that is the kind of person to whom James is referring here.

The interpretation followed by Zodhiates would obviously explain the phrase 'knowing to do good' – these Christian businessmen knew that they *ought* to bring God into the centre of their planning. But there is another obvious possibility. It seems to me that the words 'Knowing to do good' have a horizontal sense. They remind me immediately of what was said of Jesus – (He) went about doing good' (Acts

10:38). If you contrast that with the fact that the phrase 'buy and sell, and get gain' showed these businessmen to be selfish and greedy, the connection becomes clear and the point obvious. These men knew what it was to do good – that is, to share with other people, to be generous. As God blessed them in their work, or gave them success in their business ventures, they knew from the example of Jesus and from the teaching of scripture that the right thing for them to do was to give to others, to share with those less fortunate than themselves, to help those in need. But they refused to do this. They hoarded up their wealth for themselves. That was their sin, and why they were condemned. Those seem to me to be valid connections between verse 17 and the verses immediately before it.

Having established the connection, let us now

2. *EMPHASISE THE COMPARISON* – that is, the comparison this verse bears to the general drift of New Testament teaching. To begin with, it is certainly clear that there is a comparison with this verse and the rest of the Epistle of James. Far from being some kind of anonymous foreign import, as some people seem to think, this is vintage James. For instance, it is James who says 'Be ye doers of the word, and not hearers only, deceiving your own selves' (1:22). It is James who scathingly condemns those who see others in need, but do nothing to help them (2:15–16). It is James who says that 'faith without works is dead' (2:26). Beyond any doubt, the verse before us is pure James.

There is also a comparison with the rest of the New Testament, and when we take this wider look, we discover that far from being peripheral, this question of sins of omission is tremendously important. Listen to Jesus, for instance, castigating the scribes and Pharisees – 'Woe to you, scribes and Pharisees, hypocrites! for you tithe mint and dill and cummin, and have neglected the weightier matters of the law, justice and mercy and faith; these you ought to have done, without neglecting the others'. (Matthew 23:23 RSV) Jesus is condemning them, not for tithing, but for *not* doing other things. They were condemned for sins of omission. Then we have the parable of the talents, told by Jesus in

Matthew 25. A man gave one of his servants five talents, another two and another one. On his master's return, the man who was given five talents was able to show an increase of five, and was rewarded accordingly. The man with two talents had also made 100% trading profit, and again his master is delighted to reward him. But the man given only one talent confesses that he did not use it at all, he just kept it buried for safety's sake. That man was roundly condemned, not for doing something wrong, but for failing to do something right. It was a sin of omission. The very next passage in Matthew 25 tells of the day of judgment, of the dividing of all men as 'sheep' and 'goats'. To the goats God says 'Depart from me, ye cursed, into everlasting fire, prepared for the devil and his angels'. (Matthew 25:41) And why were they rejected and cast out? Are we told that they had murdered or committed adultery, or robbery or some other grievous offence? No! They were condemned for the *ommision of good deeds*. They gave the hungry no food, they gave the thirsty no drink, they gave the stranger no shelter, they gave the naked no clothing, and they gave the prisoner no company. They were condemned for sins of omission.

In fact, we could go one step further than that and say that everyone who is lost, everyone who fails to become a Christian, everyone who ultimately misses heaven, does so because of a sin of omission. Talking about His coming into the world to save sinners, Jesus said, 'He that believes in him is not condemned; he who does not believe is condemned already, because he does not believe in the name of the only Son of God' (John 3:18 RSV). That is a sin of omission – the sin of not believing. Jesus says that when a man is lost it is because he has not believed on Him. This whole question of sins of omission is not, therefore, just a casual and unimportant one, something that is out on the circumference. It is something that effects a man's salvation. Men are lost by a sin of omission. The man who does not repent toward God and believe on the Lord Jesus Christ is lost for ever. Although no man is saved by good works, he is lost by failing to do this good work of repentance and faith. Then, as Christians, our discipleship is defective if there are these sins of omission. Jesus went about doing good, and we are meant to do likewise. That is the plain, positive and practical teaching of James.

Having established the connection and emphasised the comparison, let us now.

3. *EXTEND THE CONTEXT*. Let us take the issue beyond the illustration of the businessmen, and beyond the examples we have noted elsewhere in the New Testament, and see it in a wider context. Firstly, notice

(1) *The responsibility inferred* – '. . . to him that knoweth to do good'. The point is surely clear. The evil here was not in just not doing that which was right; it was in not doing that which they *knew* to be right. The real fault was not that it was ignorant sin, but that it was informed sin. They knew what the right thing was and they deliberately ignored it. Notice the way in which this truth is brought out by Jesus in John 9. He had been teaching about the terrible reality of spiritual blindness in the world. The Pharisees were incensed at this and they asked Him whether He was daring to suggest that they were blind, with all of their background, tradition and knowledge. To this challenge Jesus replied 'If you were blind, you would have no sin; but because you now claim to have sight, your sin remains. If you were blind, you would not be guilty of sin; but because you insist, "We do see clearly", you are unable to escape your guilt'.

The same truth is vividly illustrated by the Apostle Paul. Speaking of ungodly mankind in general, he refers to those 'who by their wickedness suppress the truth. For what can be known about God is plain to them, because God has shown it to them. Ever since the creation of the world His invisible nature, namely, His eternal power and deity, has been clearly perceived in the things that have been made. So they are without excuse; 'for although they *knew* God they did not honour him as God or give thanks to him' (Romans 1 : 18–21 RSV). Again, the point is very clear. These men knew about God. They had come to some kind of intellectual undersatnding about the existence of God and in the light of that truth they refused to honour God or to give thanks to Him. In other words, the heart of their spiritual crime was a sin of omission.

Question 14 in the Shorter Catechism asks 'What is sin?' and the answer given is this – 'Sin is any want of conformity unto, or transgression of, the law of God'. Notice that the answer begins with 'any want of conformity unto . . . the law of God'. Sins of omission! In certain editions of the Catechism the illustration given of that point is the illustration of the priest in the story of the Good Samaritan, the man who passed by on the other side. The interesting thing to notice is that as we understand the story, the man's crime was not that he passed by – walking along the road is not a sin! – but that he knew from his reading the scriptures that it was right to help someone in need, and he failed to do so.

Here is the responsibility inferred – the responsibility of knowledge, and especially knowledge of the scriptures. A. W. Tozer, one of the most penetrating American writers and preachers of recent years once wrote 'The purpose behind all doctrine is to secure moral action'. In other words, if we read the Bible and it does not get further than our heads, then there is something wrong; it is not profitable. The Bible is meant to go beyond our brain cells; it is meant to reach into the blood stream of our life. Peter's last words included the command that we should 'grow in grace, and in the knowledge of our Lord and Saviour Jesus Christ' (2 Peter 3:18). To grow in knowledge without growing in grace is to increase our responsibility and diminish our reward.

Having noted the responsibility inferred, let us turn to

(2) *The range involved* – 'to him that knoweth *to do good* . . .'. No particular good is mentioned in the phrase, so the points I am going to make will, I confess, be arbitrary. They are chosen out of many. Every good that we know to do, we ought to do. Here are some of them that fit the principle very well. It is important to look at them because it will help us to focus the truth in some down to earth detail. Some years ago I read Dr W. E. Sangster's booklet 'A Spiritual Checkup' on the very day when I was going to the dotcor for a physical examination. There is no doubt as to which was the more demanding! The Methodist was much more searching than the medical doctor that day! May I suggest that you have a checkup *now*? Here are some of the areas you should examine.

Firstly, *prayer*. When Jesus told the story about the importunate widow He did so for one reason, 'that men ought always to pray, and not to faint' (Luke 18:1), or, as the Revised Standard Version puts it, 'and not lose heart'. How do you measure up to that? Ignoring other possible defects in your prayer life for the moment, are you guilty of praying and giving up? What about that missionary for whom you promised to pray? – or that sick friend who still has a need of prayer after many weeks, months or even years of being in great need? – or that person's financial need? – that church member's spiritual need? – or that unsaved friend, relative or neighbour? Have you given up praying? Have you lost heart? Jesus said we 'ought always to pray'; not that we should be praying all the time, but that we should continue to pray and not give up and lose heart. We live in an age of short term commitments, crash courses and push buttons. Have you lost out on the costly responsibility to wrestle with God in prayer? Are you guilty of the sin of omission here?

Secondly, *meditation on the scriptures*. I do not mean Bible reading, because I assume in normal circumstances that every Christian reads his Bible daily. But for too many people, reading the Bible is just a daily ritual. It is formal, cold, mechanical. I believe that there would be a revolution in the life of the church if Christians made an honest examination in this particular area and had a fresh approach to the scriptures altogether, one that led them to meditate on the Word and not just to read it. Dr A. T. Pierson once said, 'If you want to understand the Bible, get on your knees and read it on your knees; or if you do not literally search it on your knees, let your soul be bowed down before God. You will learn more in one hour of prayerful communion with the Spirit than in a thousand years in all the schools of human culture'. The Psalmist says of the righteous man 'his delight is in the law of the Lord, and on His law he meditates day and night' (Psalm 1:2 RSV). Not just reading, you notice, but meditation. How much do you meditate on God's Word? Are you just having a sort of pre-digested breakfast each day, prepared by somebody else in the coolness of their studies some many months before? The age in which we live does not allow for hours of concentrated thought every day before we get out to work, but somehow or another our lives have got to be organised in such a way that we allow ourselves time for greater meditation on the scriptures.

Thirdly, *relationships in the home*. One of the most sinister elements in the tragedy of our 20th Century is the breakup of home life. All the modern social structures that we have today tend to the disintegration of the home, yet God-centred homes are what Colin Kerr called, in the title of his book 'The Bulwarks of a Nation'. In Colossians 3, Paul gives us what has been called 'An Ideal Home Exhibition', a list of personal relationship built on true Christian foundations. The husband's relationship to the wife, for instance – 'Husbands, love your wives, and be not bitter against them' (v. 19). It is so easy for a husband to be unsympathetic towards his wife, to feel that her problems are so trivial compared with his. After all he is responsible for running the whole world, isn't he? – whereas she has such footling responsibilities by comparison. It is possible for the husband to be casual, unconcerned. Husbands, the Bible says that we should love our wives and be not bitter against them.

Then there is the wife's relationship to the husband – 'Wives, submit yourselves unto your own husbands, as it is fit in the Lord' (v. 18). We hear a great deal today about 'Women's Lib'. The Bible seems, rather, to emphasise what we might call 'Women's sub' – the wife's proper submission to her husband – but that is not quite so popular today! The spirit of the world has infiltrated into the home here and the results are disastrous. For a woman to lead the home and dominate the partnership is contrary to the Divine decree. There is no question of the wife being inferior in any way. Beyond any question she is the husband's rightful equal. She has all the wonderful liberties given to every believer in Christ, but as William Hendrikson puts it in his commentary on Colossians 'In His sovereign wisdom God has made the human pair in such a manner that it is natural for the husband to lead and for the wife to follow'. When that order is disturbed then there is disaster in the home.

Next we have the parents' relationship to their children – 'Fathers, provoke not your children to anger, lest they be discouraged' (v. 21). The word for 'fathers' might in fact legitimately be translated 'parents', but perhaps the use of 'fathers' draws out a necessary emphasis. The mother's responsibility towards the child could properly be summed up in the word 'love', and is obvious in its day to day out-working. But perhaps the point about fathers is particularly relevant in the busy and bustling world in which we live today. It is so subtly easy for the father to think, 'My job is the bread-winning, and my wife's job is to raise the children'. It is so easy to think of children as a headache and not as a heritage, a problem and not as a privilege. But the Bible points us in other directions. The husband has a responsibility to love his children, to spend time with them, to accommodate their mistakes, to be patient to them, to be kind to them, not to treat them in such a way that they become fretful and discouraged. Hendrikson again puts it very well – 'Fathers should create an atmosphere which will make obedience an easy and natural matter, namely the atmosphere of love and confidence'. Are you a father? And if so, where do you stand in this issue?

Then we have the children's relationship to their parents – 'Children, obey your parents in all things: for this is well pleasing unto the Lord' (v. 20). We live in an age of restless-ness, revolt and revolution, and so often in the home. I find it very challenging to notice that one of the signs of the last days, given to us in the scriptures, that children will be 'disobedient to parents' (2 Timothy 3:2). Insofar as we see an increase in our country of rampant disobedience to parents, we see a sign of the last days. This juvenile revolt strikes the most terrible blows at the harmony and the happiness of the home and at the child's own well being. If only some of us responsible within and beyond our families for instructing children would remember this, and get the message across!

Fourthly, *the question of giving*. It has been said that the unconsecrated wealth of Christians is the greatest hindrance to Christian progress. I have been able to look at that issue from so many angles – as an 'ordinary' Christian in the pew, as a voluntary worker in a Christian organisation, as a full-

time preacher dependant through a society on the gifts of
others for my own income and as a council member of a
number of Christian organisations. The result is that I am
inclined to agree with that assessment. Unconsecrated Christian wealth is *one* of the greatest hindrances, humanly
speaking, to the bringing in of the Kingdom of God. Many
solidly evangelical Christians have never honestly faced up
to the issue of tithing for instance. Have you? Have you
come to a settled conviction about the meaning of Malachi
3:8-10? Look it up *now!* – and do not turn from it until
you are sure that you understand it and will obey it. When
did you last sit down and prayerfully examine your steward-
ship in the light of your total (and perhaps steadily increasing) income, the urgency of the hour, and the cross of
Calvary, where the One who was rich became poor, that you
through His poverty might be made rich?

Lastly, *practical help to other people*. The Bible exhorts
us – 'Do not neglect to do good and to share what you have,
for such sacrifices are pleasing to God' (Hebrews 13:16
RSV); and again, 'As we have therefore opportunity, let us
do good unto all men, especially unto them who are of the
household of faith' (Galatians 6:10). We live in a world of
need, pressure and hardship. There is a huge grey mass of
normal, day to day, average human need all around us, and
as Christians we should be turned towards it and involved
in it. We should be known as those who are always the first
to lend a helping hand, to comfort a sufferer, to run an
errand. And remember the impact here – that to know a
thing is good and right to do, and to fail to do it, is to us,
sin. Remember, too, James's point about the brevity of life.
Does that not add an urgency to all of these things that we
have been saying? It has been said that delayed obedience
is disobedience, and we need to be as urgent about our
response to God's revealed will to us as Christians, as we
urge sinners to be about their response to the gospel.

Perhaps these words, though a little light in touch, will
help to bring the whole point home –

He was going to be all that a mortal could be – tomorrow.
No-one would be kinder or braver than he – tomorrow.
A friend who was troubled and weary, he knew,
Who'd be glad of a lift – and he needed it too;
On him he would call and see what he could do – tomorrow.

Each morning he'd stack up the letters he'd write –
    tomorrow.
And think of the folk he would fill with delight – tomorrow.
It was too bad indeed, he was busy today,
And hadn't a moment to stop on his way;
More time he would have to give others he'd say – tomorrow.

The greatest of mortals this man would have been –
    tomorrow.
The world would have known him, had he ever seen
    tomorrow.
But the fact is, he died, and he faded from view,
And all that was left when his living was through,
Was a mountain of things he intended to do – tomorrow!

The lesson is not philosophical, but practical; not general, but personal; not negative, but positive; not casual, but urgent – 'Therefore to him that knoweth to do good, and doeth it not, to him it is sin'.